OPENING GOVERNMENT

TRANSPARENCY AND ENGAGEMENT
IN THE INFORMATION AGE

OPENING GOVERNMENT

TRANSPARENCY AND ENGAGEMENT
IN THE INFORMATION AGE

EDITED BY JOHN WANNA
AND SAM VINCENT

PRESS

the Australia and New Zealand
School of Government

Published by ANU Press
The Australian National University
Acton ACT 2601, Australia
Email: anupress@anu.edu.au
This title is also available online at press.anu.edu.au

Contents

Part 3: Transparency and data management

Abbreviations

ANZSOG	Australia and New Zealand School of Government
API	application programming interface
ATO	Australian Taxation Office
BCG	Boston Consulting Group
BPS	Better Public Services
CIO	chief information officer
DHS	Department of Human Services
fMRI	functional magnetic resonance imaging
FOI	freedom of information
GCDO	government chief digital officer
GFC	global financial crisis
GP	general practitioner
GST	Goods and Services Tax
ICT	information and communications technology
MCA	multi-category appropriation
MMP	mixed-member proportional
MP	Member of Parliament
NEET	not engaged in education, employment or training
NIMBY	not in my backyard
OECD	Organisation for Economic Co-operation and Development
QCET	Queensland Community Engagement Trial
SES	Senior Executive Service
UK	United Kingdom
UKIP	UK Independence Party
US	United States

Contributors

Tanja Aitamurto

Tanja Aitamurto is a postdoctoral scholar in the Department of Management Science and Engineering at Stanford University, where she works in the Crowdsourced Democracy Team. Previously, she worked as a postdoctoral Brown Fellow and as Deputy Director of the Brown Institute for Media Innovation at Stanford. Tanja has designed and developed several online platforms and processes for crowdsourced journalism and policymaking, and advised local and national governments in participatory policymaking projects.

David Bartlett

David Bartlett was the 43rd premier of Tasmania, from 2008 until 2011. During his parliamentary career, he also held the portfolios of Minister for Education and Skills, Minister for Innovation, Science and Technology, and Attorney-General. Since leaving parliament, David has been working with regional economies, industry sectors and communities across Australia to prepare strategies for maximising economic and social renewal underpinned by broadband and digital technologies. David is now a Director of Explor Consulting.

Ron Ben-David

Ron Ben-David has served as Chairperson of the Essential Services Commission of Victoria since 2008. The Commission is Victoria's economic regulator and covers multiple sectors, including electricity and gas, water, port, freight rail, taxi, tow truck, and local government. Ron has written and presented on a wide range of topics covering regulation, governance and economics. His papers regarding the energy sector have largely focused on the competitiveness of the retail energy market.

Paula Bennett

Paula Bennett is a former deputy prime minister of New Zealand, and held the Cabinet portfolios of State Services, Women, Tourism, Police, and Climate Change Issues. She became the Member of Parliament (MP) for Upper Harbour in 2014 after having served as MP for Waitakere for six years. She has previously been Minister of Social Development, Minister of Local Government, Social Housing, and Associate Minister of Tourism and Finance. She is currently New Zealand's deputy opposition leader.

Philip Evans

Philip Evans is a senior partner in the Boston Office of the Boston Consulting Group (BCG) and a BCG Fellow. He is a frequent speaker on technology and strategy at industry, corporate and academic conferences and has given keynote addresses at conferences convened by Bill Gates, Michael Milken, TED, the Seoul Digital Forum and the World Economic Forum.

Oliver Hartwich

Oliver Hartwich is the executive director of The New Zealand Initiative, an independent public policy think tank supported by chief executives of major New Zealand businesses. Before joining the initiative, he was a Research Fellow at the Centre for Independent Studies in Sydney, the chief economist at Policy Exchange London and an adviser in the UK House of Lords.

Dominik Hierlemann

Dominik Hierlemann, an expert in public participation and democracy, is a senior project manager at the Bertelsmann Stiftung, Germany's leading think tank in the field of education and democracy. Dominik was the project leader of the Citizens' Forum in 2011, initiated by the Federal President, which has been the biggest project in the field of citizen engagement in Germany. Since then, he has created and carried out multiple civic engagement projects with the Federal President and the Chancellor, Angela Merkel.

Marie Johnson

Marie Johnson is the managing director and chief digital officer at the Centre for Digital Business. She has extensive senior executive experience in the public and private sectors in Australia and internationally in technology and innovation. As a federal government agency chief information officer, chief technology architect and services transformation strategist, Marie has delivered significant technology, innovation and digital services transformation programs across taxation, business, social services, payments and immigration operations in the Australian Government.

E. Allan Lind

E. Allan Lind is the James L. Vincent Distinguished Professor of Leadership, Fuqua School of Business, Duke University. His research interests include psychology of fairness, reactions to authority, organisational behaviour, and citizen and stakeholder reactions to government policies and regulations. Prior to joining Duke, Allan did policy research on law and public policy at the US Federal Judicial Center, the RAND Corporation and the American Bar Foundation.

Colin MacDonald

Colin MacDonald is chief executive of New Zealand's Department of Internal Affairs, Secretary for Internal Affairs, Secretary for Local Government and Government Chief Digital Officer (GCDO). In his GCDO role, Colin is the information and communications technology (ICT) function leader for government and acts with the authority of a Cabinet directive to lead the transformation of government ICT to support radically transformed public services. Colin is also responsible for the success of the government's Better Public Services Result 10 initiative: 'New Zealanders can complete their transactions with government easily in a digital environment'.

Stephen Mayne

Stephen Mayne is a business journalist by profession who spent 10 years on daily newspapers before founding Australia's best-known independent ezine, *Crikey* (crikey.com.au), in 2000. He is a former political staffer and local government councillor who also pursues shareholder advocacy as a director of the Australian Shareholders' Association and campaigns broadly for transparency and accountability across the media, business and political sectors.

Erma Ranieri

Erma Ranieri is Commissioner for Public Sector Employment, Office for the Public Sector, South Australia. She oversees multiple sector-wide reform programs including Change@SouthAustralia, executive development and leadership, and developing a sustainable approach to workforce management.

Tamati Shepherd

Tamati Shepherd is a former chief digital officer, Department of Human Services (DHS). His portfolio of responsibility focuses strongly on government digital and transformation programs, innovation and design, which also included the *myGov* digital service. In his previous role at the DHS, Tamati was responsible for leading the development of the business case, which included establishing the current Welfare Payment Infrastructure Transformation Programme. He is currently a partner at professional services organisation EY.

Anne Tiernan

Anne Tiernan is Dean (Engagement) for the Griffith Business School, Griffith University. A political scientist with earlier careers in government in the Commonwealth and Queensland, and in teaching and consulting, Anne's research focuses on the work of governing. Her scholarly interests include Australian politics and governance, policy advice, executive studies, policy capacity, federalism and intergovernmental coordination. Anne consults regularly to Australian governments at all levels.

Sam Vincent

Sam Vincent is commissioning editor at the Australia and New Zealand School of Government.

John Wanna

John Wanna is the Sir John Bunting Chair of Public Administration in the Australia and New Zealand School of Government and Professor in the School of Politics and International Relations, College of Arts and Social Sciences, The Australian National University.

Introduction

1

Opening government: Transparency and engagement in the information age

John Wanna

Transparency promotes accountability and provides information for citizens about what their government is doing. Information maintained by the Federal Government is a national asset. My administration will take appropriate action … to disclose information rapidly in forms that the public can readily find and use.

– US President Barack Obama, memo to Heads of Departments and Agencies on Transparency and Open Government, January 2009

We now have technologies that offer unprecedented opportunities for the direct and secure communication of information. More importantly, they provide us with unprecedented opportunities for interaction. And they are woven into everyday life so inextricably that, to the younger members of our community especially, they have become invisible. They offer a huge potential to party organisation and for party democracy, and at the same time fundamentally change expectations of participation, engagement and responsiveness.

– Senator John Faulkner, 'Public Pessimism, Political Complacency: Restoring Trust, Reforming Labor', Inaugural Address to the Light on the Hill Society, October 2014

... the Government commits to actively releasing high value public data ... [held] on behalf of the New Zealand public. We release it to enable the private and community sectors to use it to grow the economy, strengthen our social and cultural fabric, and sustain the environment. We release it to encourage business and community involvement in government decision-making ... the Government's Open Data Initiative ... is one of a range of measures driving better use of public data, while upholding high ethical and privacy standards. Measures include investing in Statistics NZ's Integrated Data Infrastructure System, establishing the Data Futures Forum and data.govt initiative ...

– NZ Declaration on Open and Transparent Government 2011 and Deputy Prime Minister Bill English, February 2015

If we are serious about promoting the benefits of digital innovation, as a government we need to improve the quality and availability of our own services. This includes opening up and releasing government data that would otherwise only be collecting dust in digital cupboards ... I am sure many of you are aware of the 2014 report by Lateral Economics which suggests that 'more vigorous open data policies could add around $16 billion per annum to the Australian economy'. Governments hold an extraordinary amount of unique data, collected directly and indirectly in the course of doing our job. It is there. We have it. But there is no point in keeping all that data stored away. It needs to be accessed, analysed, understood, used and reused. Since the Government was elected [Sept 2013], the number of datasets available on data.gov.au has increased from 514 to more than 5200: a tenfold increase ... But the Government's open data focus is not just about opening more and more datasets. It is also about opening high-value datasets.

– Communications Minister Malcolm Turnbull, March 2015

APS employees need to ensure that they fully understand the APS Values and Code of Conduct and how they apply to official and unofficial communications. If in doubt, they should consider carefully whether to comment and what to say; consult their agency's policies; seek advice from someone in authority in their agency; or consult the Ethics Advisory Service in the Australian Public Service Commission.

– Circular 2012/1: Revisions to the Australian Public Service Commission's guidance on making public comment and participating online (social media)

To fulfil the Australia and New Zealand School of Government's (ANZSOG) mandate with its stakeholder governments, the school hosts annual conferences that explore significant topics of import to good governance in the Australasian public sphere. These in turn are published as monographs, under the auspices of ANU Press. Previous volumes have tackled complex issues including implementation and project management in the public sector; collaborative governance and working collaboratively with non-government organisations and the 'not-for-profit' third sector; inter-jurisdictional and intergovernmental policy relations; social and economic responses to managing the global financial crisis (GFC); attracting political interest in delivering policy reform and making it 'stick'; citizen engagement and putting citizens first in service delivery; learning from disaster management to 'future-proof' the state and society, and enhance resilience and risk management; responding in innovative, strategic and productive ways to the post-GFC fiscal crisis facing present-day governments who have imposed austerity agendas and tight budgets across their areas of responsibility; and, most recently, leveraging the capacities of the public sector to increase national prosperity and wellbeing. In all of these publications, ANZSOG has striven to be relevant and engaging to governments, public sector executives, policy practitioners and service deliverers.

Opening Government: Transparency and Engagement in the Information Age, the latest in the series, is similarly aimed at a compelling issue of immediate relevance to governments, their governance relationships and citizenry engagement. It explores new horizons and scenarios for better governance in the context of the new information age, focusing on the potentials and pitfall for governments (and governance more broadly) operating in the new, information-rich environment. It asks what are the challenges to our governing traditions and practices in the new information age, and where can better outcomes be expected using future technologies. It explores the fundamental ambiguities extant in opening up government, with governments intending to become far more transparent in providing information and in information sharing, but also more motivated to engage with other data sources, data systems and social technologies.

In one sense, we are at an important crossroads with various future paths available to tread. ANZSOG and its principal stakeholders are also conscious that this is an agenda with which most Western societies and their governments are presently wrestling and will do so for some further decades to come. But at a time when Western governments and their public managers are grappling with how the new information age can contribute to the provision of effective, efficient, open and accountable government, which we (may) all value, we are also aware that the liberal democratic values that promote transparency and disclosure, authentic engagement with clients and citizens, and greater trust and legitimacy between governments and their constituencies are becoming particularly fragile. If governments are genuine about opening government up (and they may have much less choice in this matter than they currently think), then it behoves them to maximise the potential of the opportunities offered and also to weigh and manage the risks well and appropriately. They must accept that this is a global social milieu they cannot control, replete with disruptive technologies, new channels of communication, new forms of interconnectivity, new information sources and new influential players.

The power asymmetries between governments and civilians are shifting dramatically, and have the potential to shift even further into the future. Socially based interactive digital technologies like social media may give way to other less digital-based technologies in the future—recognition technologies, thought identification, telepathic communication or detection, self-calibrating information management systems (driverless vehicles or trains, automated transport management systems). The present highly individualised, multi-channelled information age is already a discursive challenge for governments and regulators (especially channelled through social media), where following the norms of 'expressive individualism', everyone's voices, thoughts, photos and videos are digitally communicated and relayed across the cyber universe, where self-indulgence and relativism rules, and bounds of inappropriateness are tested. Future technologies and new forms of expressivity that bring other forms of social or individual empowerment (choice, discretion, assertiveness, resistance) will pose additional ethical dilemmas (e.g. abusiveness, shaming, cyber-bullying, trolling etc.). Governments will have to cope with the libertarian and emancipatory possibilities of social media and other interactive technologies.

Many technological innovations are conceived as intrinsic 'means' and neutral platforms that are indiscriminate as to ends, and therefore open to good and bad uses, virtuous or evil ends. This is as true for nuclear physics as for the internet, as it is for Facebook and the smartphone. Smart technologies are adopted by and as useful to the terrorist, crime gang, anarchist protester, tax-evader and paedophile as they are for community-minded purposes, social clubs and friendship circles, personal entertainment and enhanced service experiences. New technologies provide new opportunities for society but also change the risk profiles, and open up new risks. So, how should governments position themselves in this information age? How will they be best able to manage the processes and consequences? And how might governments exploit the new possibilities to enhance the quality of their outputs and improve outcomes?

The contributors to this volume explore and address these issues under six key themes:

1. Shaping (and reshaping) our democracies and democratic outcomes in the new information age—exploring how our public, private and community sectors can better respond to the potentialities of the information age.
2. Using transparency to rebuild or enhance legitimacy and trust relationships between governments and citizens, and contributing to greater confidence and assurance.
3. Engaging in authentic engagement through opening up policy processes to improve the public sector's capacity to deliver public value and meet rising citizen and community needs.
4. Exploring how we can better share administrative data for effective outcomes, integrate additional and non-governmental data sources and gain real benefits from managing and interrogating 'big data'.
5. Reflecting after nearly 40 years on whether we have got the balance right with freedom of information (FOI) laws, especially as most of our jurisdictions have now adopted default disclosure provisions and open access regimes.
6. Finding ways to use rapidly evolving digital systems and other transformational technologies to improve policy advice and public management and the quality delivered services.

The over-riding intention of *Opening Government* is to traverse practical and applicable ways in which governments can best respond to the ongoing challenges—to find practical ways to gain more value from these opportunities and from our best mix of inputs, resources and relationships. But this is not to neglect the theoretical and conceptual underpinnings associated with the opening government agenda, which will be examined in many of the following chapters. Hopefully, the new information age can reshape what we do, how we do it and the quality with which it is done. The aim as always is to deliver effective outcomes across our various domains and changing responsibilities of public policy. It is a challenge we hope to share with you, so that you can take back these concepts, ideas and practical ways of doing the business of government under today's more productive imperatives.

Westminster's reluctant transformation – from secrecy to relative openness

Westminster and open information were traditionally uneasy fellow travellers, and some might argue even antithetical. The antipathy to openness was humorously captured by *Yes Minister*'s Sir Humphrey when he asserted open government was a *non sequitur*; one could have openness *or* government but not *both* at the same time. Traditional Westminster (pre-dating mass democracy) was essentially derived from crown prerogative. It prided itself on being an efficient form of government, loosely based on consent rather than consultation or direct input from the populace. Its strong executives, with command over parliaments, ruled by convention and were largely unconstrained by countervailing forces (or checks and balances) until relatively recently in its long history. When Walter Bagehot (1867) put his finger on the 'efficient secret' of English government, he meant that it was very amenable to political action and rule from behind the scenes, unconstrained by hard and fast constitutional impediments or rigidities.

Over many centuries, Westminster operated on the basis of executive decree, supported by norms of secrecy, confidentiality and minimal disclosure of rationales for action/inaction; governments would readily announce decisions once taken but rarely explain or disclose how they came to the decision-making.[1] Despite its reluctant embrace of elected representational government from the 19th century onwards, Westminster remained shrouded in royal mystique and crown privilege. It produced a system of government in Britain and a few settler dominions where the political culture insisted elitist governments 'knew best' and should be left alone to govern until the next election, and where the populace was characterised by a 'subject political culture', less motivated by participation or aggressive self-interest (Almond and Verba 1963).

---

1   Some other Western countries had fashioned political systems comparatively more open than Westminster, notably the United States, Sweden, Denmark and Switzerland.

Westminster structured a fundamental informational asymmetry between a powerful executive government and the official opposition, media outlets and its citizenry or residents (in many instances, even parliament did not know what the executive was up to, and the executive composed the majority of the legislature). These cultures prevailed with few challenges largely until the post-war years, when many factors combined to engineer change—growing international compulsion through declarations and treaties, the United Nations, growing domestic and international legalism, social mobility and mass education, new technologies and the arrival of mass communication, the erosion of party loyalties and rising distrust in governments/politicians, increased media scrutiny, democratic pressures and the growth of pressure groups, and the after-effects of major government scandals.

But alongside these developments, a more sceptical society emerged with sections of the population alienated from the political system (Norris 1999). Gradually, governments also came to view greater openness more positively, but still sceptically—especially with the adoption of FOI provisions and administrative law more generally (ironically, the UK was the last Westminster system to embrace FOI, as recently as the Blair Government).

The rise of the new information age (probably from the early 1990s) began to change the landscape, at first evolutionary but then much more radically. Some new technologies such as the arrival of desktop PCs and new communication media (such as email and Facebook) were eagerly adopted by governments and changed the ways government internally operated and communicated, dispensing with the need to maintain paper files and formal memos. These early communicative technologies were quick and convenient and tended to reinforce old modes of government rather than challenge them. Governments initially simply gained more computing, calculating and communicating capacities—and they seized the opportunities to gain more information from their populations, greater integration of information sources and more analytical capabilities to analyse the collected data (especially important for taxation, financial monitoring, welfare administration, people movements etc.).

But the speed of technological change escalated markedly and, as far more individualistic and atomistic technological systems emerged that could build into social networks and wage social media campaigns, old asymmetries in information richness quickly shifted, placing enormous pressures on our political and democratic systems and cultures of governance. On the one hand, these new social media technologies suddenly offered the prospect of greater democratic empowerment and citizen participation in decision-making; but, on the other hand, they also unleashed new forms of enslavement, apathy, faddish following and herd instincts. Not only were previous imbalances in information access suddenly realigned, but entirely new areas of information, knowledge and communication were flourishing in which citizens (individually and collectively) were much more in control of the framing of ideas/attitudes and control of the content conveyed, especially through social media and social networking platforms.

Not only were ordinary people empowered but many of the new channels were anonymous or virtually so. These socially empowering technologies were soon forcing governments to react—at extreme levels, protesters were soon using social media to organise mass riots, but more prosaically significant sections of society were gaining their knowledge and information not from government sources but from each other. Government's near-monopoly of information provision and analysis was contested by new (non-state) sources of information, new analytical capacities in the community and non-government sectors, and new networks of communication with influence and opinion-shaping capacities largely beyond the scope (and sometimes knowledge) of government. Although modern governments responded with the rapid escalation of the 'surveillance state' governments had largely lost control of the initiative in the new information age.

In responding to the new information age, governments tended to be 'behind the game' playing catch-up. By the 2010s, most governments across our many jurisdictions in Australia and New Zealand had formally adopted 'open government' policies and endorsed the findings of relevant taskforces and investigative reports, and then enshrined the sentiments on websites (often leaving them unattended or frozen in time from that moment on). These 'open government' declarations talked of the benefits of transparency, the digitalisation of data and public release and disclosure of information, and the huge potential that could accrue to the economy through governments sharing data sources with business and the community. For instance, the Commonwealth Government announced in 2010 that:

> The Australian Government's support for openness and transparency in Government has three key principles:

Informing: strengthening citizen's rights of access to information, establishing a pro-disclosure culture across Australian Government agencies including through online innovation, and making government information more accessible and usable;

Engaging: collaborating with citizens on policy and service delivery to enhance the processes of government and improve the outcomes sought; and

Participating: making government more consultative and participative (Commonwealth of Australia, 2010).

These are laudable ideals but are they being actively implemented? Are they really changing the internal and external cultural practices of governments, their administrative practices and their interactions with citizens? The following sections examine the value of transparency and openness (as well as some limitations); the prospects for sharing administrative data and how far governments will be able to overcome the reluctance to share their data sets; the possibilities of new technologies in enhancing authentic citizen engagement; and the reactions of governments to existing FOI regimes including the warnings of some that FOI has had perverse consequences.

The value of transparency (and some risks or challenges to its virtues)

> Transparency enables information flows that enhance policy decision-making and program design.
>
> – Professor Gary Banks, Dean ANZSOG/former Chair of Productivity Commission.

Transparency in public life is a fundamental attribute of accountability and oversight. Transparency implies the disclosure of information held or collected by government on which it may base its decisions, administer and operate its affairs, seek to impact on the community and establish priorities. Information can include administrative or processing data, financial accounts and resource allocation, planning and policy priorities, information collected on citizens or groups, and information involving other governments where some joint arrangement is open to scrutiny. Good governance flourishes not only where citizens have *rights* of access to information, procedures and documentation, but also where a *culture* of openness and accountability permeate the relations between governments and citizens. There is a huge literature on the need, value and normative scope of transparency going back centuries and including many of the great political philosophers and jurists of their age.

In recent times, although governments have formally endorsed the principle of transparency to better inform citizens, build trust and provide assurance, its adoption or realisation will be predictably on government's terms. Arguably transparency in itself is a double-edged sword, but not necessarily with equally sharp sides. The comparable status of the positives clearly outweighs any negatives, but both sides should be given some consideration. On the positive side transparency can be:

- A **virtue**—a normative objective, noble ideal, something to aspire to, to better inform citizens and interest groups; it is a fundamental aspect of legitimacy and trust between the government and the governed.

- An effective (and efficient) **enabler**—promoting better ways of making policy, adopting good practice, providing a level playing field open to all with transparent rules and information, allowing more effective and efficient policies because everyone has access to information on which decisions are based and the assumptions informing those decisions.

- An improved dimension of **accountability**—promoting public disclosure, public insight into decision-making, scrutiny and evaluation, and democratic oversight; it provides a robust way of exposing information, policy announcements and analysis to critical scrutiny and contestability; it can also function to impress a self-imposed discipline on governments (e.g. over performance targets, or specific policy commitments).

- A promoter of **confidence and assurance**—contributing to the maintenance of confidence and trust in public institutions, for the legitimacy of their decisions (e.g. courts) or policy frameworks (governments), allowing the community to ascertain whether governing institutions have performed fairly and legitimately or delivered on their commitments or promises.

However, transparency involves certain challenges and risks to government (and occasionally to the community more generally). Transparency can also:

- Impose risks for governments when they want to or have to negotiate in confidence to secure agreements (e.g. the Trans-Pacific Partnership negotiations), or when they wish to ration services but do not want to cause moral panic in explicitly divulging the dimensions of the rationing. Governments may wish to prioritise access to services (e.g. health services) without necessarily being explicit as to their rationing logics.

- Make it harder to deliver candid and frank and fearless advice to government (from officials but also from non-government actors who may choose to make inputs or lobby for outcomes) when analysts know that the information they provide will be released. The prospect of disclosure can also make it harder for public agencies to undertake basic research that could be politically sensitive—for instance, the Australian Treasury conducted confidential research into the affordability of home ownership for first home buyers to inform their advisory functions, yet were challenged to release the sensitive information—one consequence may be that senior officials conclude that it is better not to ask such questions or conduct such sensitive research in the future.

- Serve to encourage certain kinds of behaviour governments do not wish to see or would seek to discourage—for instance, governments do not prevent modest gift giving but do not provide transparent information on the limits of monetary gifts citizens can give to family and friends, overt transparency could be seen to be detrimental to good public policy in gift giving; similarly, governments often choose to be economical with the truth over the extent or upper limits of tax concessions for fear of encouraging greater concessionary claims.

- More open information systems may encourage governments to engage in subterfuge and political spin more than otherwise, avoiding real issues of attempting to distract public scrutiny from the actual data (government announcements and ministerial statements in relation to Australia's offshore detention regime may be an instance here). Simulated transparency and political spin may be a function of greater openness.

- Transparency can reduce flexibility for governments and impede their capacity to adapt to changing circumstances—for instance, declared renewable energy targets can create expectations among the community and industry providers, but if governments consider it prudent to change these targets the transparency of the process can stymie their intentions and possibly exacerbate the unintended consequences for those involved.

- Finally, there is a divulgence risk if governments are obliged to release information they consider best kept confidential; where there are serious arguments about the negative consequences of release—this could be sensitive information (residential locations of paedophiles or major criminals, or infection rates for hospitals or the insurance risk for GPs and medical specialists), inconsistent or confused information (location of asbestos properties, types of environmental data) or commercial information (release of information revealing intellectual property or foreign-owned property registers).

Hence, transparency is an aspirational ideal, but not always free from risks or unintended consequences. So the questions we might ask: Are the government and the community satisfied that the degree of transparency is appropriate and optimal for social outcomes? What opportunities and dilemmas for public sector managers does transparency entail, and how can these officials manage transparency appropriately?

Using openness to improve authentic engagement with the community

Governments have long talked about improving meaningful engagement with the community, probably dating back to the 1970s; but arguably far less progress has been actually achieved than expected—and much of what passes for 'engagement' can be perfunctory or confected. Technological developments have more recently facilitated the capacities of government bodies to engage over policy issues and matters of operational administration. The new information age and a new willingness to be more transparent does allow for more authentic and deeper forms of engagement with the community and citizens.

But also, engagement is about trust and nurturing greater collective benefits or value. And it applies both ways—the trust the community places in government but also the trust government has in the capacities and wisdoms of the community. Ethical and accountable leadership will involve investments in greater and more meaningful cultures of engagement. Evidence of distrust is markedly apparent: when UK Professor of Computer Science Dame Wendy Hall heard that a large Australian federal government department had appointed a senior official called a 'social media manager' who monitored and edited public comments on the department's site, said 'I don't think you get it here in the Australian government' (Hall 2013). The instinctive desire to control and sanction is a legacy of statism perhaps best consigned to the history books.

Certainly, transparency and openness can serve to better inform the community before specific consultations or engagement exercises are undertaken. We can give the public various scenarios or alternative propositions to contemplate, we can provide them with information on the consequences of decisions, the costs, opportunity costs and commitment requirements for them to consider before making input into decision-making. But while the technical possibilities for doing this already exist, we are yet far from this ideal. People in any polity routinely come into contact with the authorities at various gatekeeping points (e.g. from birth, starting school, hospital admission, gaining a tax file number), and we still think of these interactions in one-dimensional terms. For example, we are seeing schools slowly introduce vaccination and dental schedules, obesity prevention and healthy eating programs. Similarly, couples intending matrimony are being offered financial and relationship counselling.

But these connections are at the thin end of the wedge. Increasingly, governments will use new technologies to deliver client-oriented 'one-stop-shop' facilities and anticipatory client journeys. Personal records will become more proactively managed and utilised to make additional services available to people (at the citizen's discretion) at these key contact points between government and the citizen. Governments and other important social organisations hold immense data banks of personal information, which we readily collect but do not use effectively to engage with citizens and improve their wellbeing.

Governments have started to use social media campaigns to increase public input into decisions and address issues in the implementation of policy or regulatory practices. You can now provide local government with feedback on local service needs (the 'fix-my-road' sites), or provide your local police with information on social media. The areas where the use of social media has most taken off for government is in the local service delivery and frontline areas of government—for example, emergency and disaster response information, or liaison between local police and the community over missing persons.

Social media has also been used to help areas of law enforcement such as with the NSW Police's management of alcohol-induced violence (and cowardly one-punch assaults) in Sydney's Kings Cross. There are examples from Australia and New Zealand of using social media to have input into national policy issues and legislative redrafting (but arguably these remain exceptions to date). For instance, the current consultation on Australian tax policy (*Re:Think* (Australian Government 2018)) is largely based on the familiar process of formal written submission, with some opportunity to receive updates on Twitter or make a comment. It often appears that the existing processes of consultation have simply been put online.

In the immediate future, there may be scope for providing new e-services through various e-government platforms, creating evolving service mixes to benefit citizens and clients, even shaping policy and distributional logistics. There is also great potential for visualisation technologies to inform and engage citizens over 'real life' issues to explain or consult over the relevant context and complexities.

Casting off the reluctance to share administrative data with the community

As mentioned above, governments collect, through a variety of sources, enormous amounts of information on their populations for various, often unconnected, reasons. Much of this information sits in silos, used for specific purposes. But much of this information is under-utilised, especially if such sources are not compounded, correlated, integrated and shared more widely in the community. Perhaps as a consequence of our Westminster legacies (and concerns over privacy), we have not generally explored how we can better share administrative data for effective outcomes. In fact, legislation generally requires that information collected under a particular statute can only be used for the specific purposes set out in the respective legislation (taxation, auditing, health records, criminal histories, welfare applications, child custody and child support). Should we maintain this rigid compartmentalisation of information—or prepare to share its potential through linking and data mixing?

There is a whole cluster of policy areas that would greatly benefit from data-sharing innovations—from intelligence gathering, to pathway programs and custodial rehabilitation, educational pedagogies, between scientific research and industry, policing strategies, land management and monitoring activities.[2] Data sharing between different jurisdictions and between internal and external stakeholders can enable policymakers to appreciate a more rounded view of citizens' needs and compare this with the combination of services they are already receiving to gauge whether programs are making a discernible difference or providing value for money (Yates 2014).

With fewer jurisdictional barriers, the New Zealand Government has experimented with this analytical approach through its longitudinal 'investment' calculations applied to service expenditures and transfers (Mintrom 2013). So the question we may need to ask ourselves in federal nations such as Australia is: how can we change the incentive structures so that relatively independent jurisdictions will more readily experiment with data-sharing initiatives, and adopt learning policy cultures? Such inter-jurisdictional sharing of data will require political and cultural shifts and greater relationships of trust. But, equally, we need to be aware that there may be potential downsides from a more open data-sharing culture, not least privacy issues and data management.

Government websites are still managed too cautiously, dominated by official information and government-sanctioned presentations and formal publications. Few are genuinely interactive; few ask users or respondents to provide feedback or indicate satisfaction with the site and its information (even sporting clubs do this!). Few have links to other sources of information across government or outside of government (and if they do, it is usually where government itself is involved—e.g. a consultative committee, a collaborative research endeavour). Although governments talk of 'big data' and 'open data', there remains much caution about linking data from different sources both internally and externally.

We have put toes in the water with initiatives such as My School or My Hospital where heavily sanctioned information is posted on sites implying some comparability, but these sites are not interactive and

---

2   We should also be aware of the political and social context within which data transparency and data sharing takes place. There is the salutary tale of the Indian government's decision to digitalise land ownership across the country—only for unscrupulous land developers to then attempt to seize communal lands or lands not held by formal title for their own aggrandisement.

users cannot post their own responses/experiences/opinions (whereas even hotels, accommodation and tourism services do this). Examples of this kind of discussion, support and feedback on services or experiences abound in commercial domains—strong evidence of people's desire to share their experiences with others. Think of travel advice, ratings of restaurants, etc. This is not to suggest that government priorities are set this way—but there must be opportunities for more interaction.

One of the structural problems with sharing data or releasing integrated data sources is that governments are likely to release only information that serves their purposes or interests, not necessarily the community's. For instance, governments do not release much hard-edged performance information or comparative analyses of program performance, and too often any basic information published is activity-related and unaudited. (But this may be because of commercial-in-confidence restrictions of the private entities involved in delivering government services?) Governments will spend time and resources compiling spending and program data on a regional or electoral basis (for their own promotional purposes), but not divulge (say) longitudinal data, future plans or comparable data across jurisdictions or between countries.

A further problem with governments is that they become preoccupied with data integrity and reliability—they are reluctant to be seen in any way to be endorsing any competing data source or interpretation that is not theirs or officially sanctioned, or could be constructed on different assumptions or criteria. There are a range of health-related websites with reputed studies, useful information and alternative treatments that are not only not condoned by government health agencies but are effectively ignored. Visualisation techniques provide a way to build simulations and scenarios, explore correlations and present data from diverse sources.

Hence, a further challenge is for governments to become more cognisant of the benefits to be gained from 'big data' and become proactive and proficient in using and managing these various data sources. Firms have been doing this already for some years, and are well down this path especially in anticipating consumer preferences. Governments are still flat-footed. A few client-based agencies are issuing individualised age-related invitations (often still by traditional forms of communications, 'snail mail', pamphlets) anticipating client needs for such things as driving licences, electoral enrolment, proclivities of certain cancers and illnesses.

It remains the case that the vast majority of datasets and data sources released publicly (and available on public websites for searching) relate to spatial and physical information (Turnbull 2015).

'Big data' offers many new possibilities for both governments and the community to benefit from the interrogation of diverse data sources to improve their information thresholds. Such data can be analysed, integrated, categorised, critiqued and evaluated. But do governments have the capacities to design and architecturally build these 'big data' systems, and manage them over time? Departments can make a big splash and look 'hip' by making grandiose open data announcements and spruiking up their websites, but to what extent are these initiatives purely symbolic? What is the take-up rate by outside organisations and community users? Does anyone use the data that is currently available and to what effect?

Investing in open data initiatives with information that governments have collected is one strategy to adopt (providing public access to data sources governments control), but we may also want to consider how the community can gain access and use the vast quantities of public data that private business entities hold—and enabling the broader community to benefit from these datasets.

As different sources of data are capable of being linked, integrated or compared, there is another important role for governments moving forward. Their role here is not to dismiss, censor or attack such data sources, but to comment on the overall quality and reliability of the data presented and, importantly, to provide expert opinion as to whether the data is appropriate for capturing a particular policy problem.

Freedom of information—or information free-for-all

FOI legislation has been in place across our jurisdictions since the early 1980s, with both the Australian Commonwealth and New Zealand introducing legislation effective from 1982; the last Australian state, Queensland, coming on board in the early 1990s. The role and benefits of FOI are widely appreciated, regularly interpreted and commented upon by the courts and in the media (Stewart 2015). Executive government has frequently asked parliament to amend the acts—sometimes to tighten access regimes, at other times to widen disclosure. Law reform commissions, administrative tribunals and courts have also played significant roles in shaping access to official information. There is now a prevailing orthodoxy based on the presumption that releasing any information is always good and in the public interest, despite its potential to discredit or embarrass government.

But after nearly 40 years, it is worth reflecting about whether we have got the balance right with FOI laws, especially as most of our jurisdictions have now adopted default disclosure provisions and open-access regimes. New Zealand has a far more open FOI regime, with executive information released immediately including cabinet decisions, information briefings and policy submissions (but what have been the consequences of such a formal release policy?). In Australia, the recent Information Publication Scheme and agency disclosure plans elevates the virtues of disclosure, perhaps unduly.

Has disclosure gone too far? Has the constant threat of disclosure changed the way governments are advised by their officials, and perhaps also reduced their candour and diluted their appetite for giving frank and fearless advice to ministers? Is the nature of the advice proffered second or third best because of the likely prospect of it emerging in the public realm? Is advice tempered by officials and constructed to be politically palatable, and are ministers now served bland advice that officials know must be made public. There are stories of ministers on both sides of the Tasman choosing only to take oral advice in strict confidence in the sanctity of their chambers—leaving no briefing history or records of decisions.

In some cases, confidential pre-meeting meetings are arranged to shape what will be decided at the formal meeting. There is ample evidence that the Red and Blue books, which were once confidential briefings presented to an incoming government, are now written with the expectation that they will be in the newspapers shortly after they are formally presented. Senior officials across many of our jurisdictions are expressing (usually privately) their concerns about the perverse effects of too much transparency on the quality of advice and institutional memory. So what does this imply for public sector managers going forward?

Accordingly, we might ask, are our FOI regimes achieving optimal performance and the expected public benefit, if governments are receiving sub-optimal advice and if ministers and officials are finding creative ways to circumvent the intent of the open access laws? Is FOI eroding the capacity of governments to deal with complex, intransigent or thorny problems? What are the consequences for various stakeholders of the public record being lessened because advice and decisions are not written down, and what specific risks to officials does this pose (e.g. the fall-out from the Home Insulation Program seemed to shift blame for design problems from ministers to officials).

Parliaments and courts may accept a certain degree of confidentiality for national security information, but are there other areas of sensitive policy deliberation that would be improved by some greater capacity to have frank internal advice? Should a Treasury department be able to research the effects of 'bracket creep' on revenue collection, or the relative affordability of housing for first home buyers, without making their investigations public? Are public agencies politically self-censoring to align with government agendas and sensitivities, and not commissioning the range and depth of analytical research?

Tensions between technological possibilities and policy capacities

Now that the tools are available to really examine what happens through new technologies, and to do more than theorise about the possibilities, can we anticipate the 'next big thing' in terms of transformational technologies and opportunities to come across the horizon? Can we find ways to use rapidly evolving digital systems and other transformational technologies to improve policy advice, public management and the quality of service delivery. And how might we proceed down these pathways? How can we avoid repeating the problems of yesteryear and find lasting solutions to our perennial problems?

Technical possibilities allow us to better inform ourselves and monitor program performance. We can use technology to improve performance measurement in real-time perspectives, and share these findings with clients, stakeholders and the general public. But these new technologies offer many more other possibilities. They are not just the monopoly of government and public sector providers (who might seek to use them purely for their own interests), but can be adopted and appropriated by non-government actors and ordinary individuals. Do we know how much demand there is from citizens for such technologies and what use they will put them to? Can we anticipate where the citizens' use of these technologies is likely to be taking us in the policy sphere, what changes are likely to accrue, and what consequences will be unleashed as a result? In short, what are the possibilities and the risks of such socially empowered performance monitoring?

One potential area to explore is the use of social media to facilitate complaint processes from the general public—enabling people to complain online, using apps or dedicated sites, which can be monitored by both delivery agencies and by accountability units such as ombudsmen's offices, tax commissioners and postal services. Indirectly, this easing of complaints processes can be recalibrated into improved service delivery at the front end.

Citizens, though, are not all equally situated or attributed. There is still a significant digital divide—between those digitally rich and digitally poor—with up to 15 per cent not connected by any technological channel or platform. This continues to raise issues of engagement, including access and equity, communication, service delivery and feedback. The digital divide is reflective of (and perhaps overlaid by) the generational divide, which can doubly disadvantage the aged over youth and neglect their voices/participation in the information age.

We should also remember that transformational technologies are novel but also highly disruptive. Large bureaucracies are often not the best placed to optimise the uptake of new technological possibilities if they threaten their modus operandi. Transformational technologies will pose threats and challenges to traditional hierarchic public organisations geared towards compliance and due diligence rather than experimentalism. And just as not all citizens are equally capable, so too not all governments or jurisdictional levels are equally capable (or resourced) to exploit the possibilities of a brave new world of information possibilities.

Conclusion

The complex relations between citizens and governments are being recalibrated through the adoption and dynamics of new technologies. But it is not a linear or unproblematic recalibration. Information and communication network platforms have much potential in changing the ways we approach policy and enhancing our democratic participation.

But how is this potential to be realised and what might be the costs or consequences of doing so? Will it cause a fundamental transformation in government–citizen/client relations, or will it merely become another instrument of possible influence and control? Already, some sections of government and the community are alert to the opportunities posed by these potentially transformational technologies; but many other sections are either showing little interest or waiting to see what transpires after others pioneer the way.

We also do not yet know what citizens will make of the new possibilities. Will they seize them and exercise greater democratic involvement, or withdraw into a cyber world of social chatter and entertainment? If more information is going to be conveyed and shared, will the availability of abundant information enhance or erode trust relations between the state and society, or will increased communication channels, and the dissemination of greater amounts of data, mix meaningful with meaningless information and pollute the well? To what extent is it likely that the more people know about the processes of government and the data stored on their behalf, the more their trust will be maintained, or are they likely to take the opposite stance, which will see citizens become more critical and become motivated by a culture of complaint? These are significant questions underlying the themes and issues of this monograph, not to mention significant questions facing governments and society into the future.

References

Almond, G. and S. Verba. 1963. *The Civic Culture: Political Attitudes and Democracy in Five Nations*. Princeton, NJ: Princeton University Press. doi.org/10.1515/9781400874569

Australian Government. 2018. *Re:Think: Better tax, better Australia*. Canberra: The Treasury. Available from bettertax.gov.au

Bagehot, W. 1867. *The English Constitution*. London: Chapman & Hall.

Commonwealth of Australia. 2010. 'Declaration of Open Government'. Department of Finance, Canberra. Available from www.finance.gov.au/blog/2010/07/16/declaration-open-government/

Hall, W. 2013. 'The Social Machine'. ANZSOG Workshop, 22 October, The Australian National University, Canberra.

Mintrom, M. 2013. 'Public Policy as Investment'. ANZSOG Occasional Paper No. 24, 18 February, Melbourne. Available from www.anzsog. edu.au/resource-library/research/public-policies-as-investments

Norris, P. 1999. *Critical Citizens: Global Support for Democratic Government.* Oxford University Press. doi.org/10.1093/0198295685.001.0001

Stewart, D. 2015. 'Assessing Access to Information in Australia: The Impact of Freedom of Information Laws on the Scrutiny and Operation of the Commonwealth Government'. In *New Accountabilities, New Challenges,* edited by J. Wanna, E. Lindquist and P. Marshall. Canberra: ANU Press. doi.org/10.22459/NANC.04.2015.04

Turnbull, M. 2015. 'The Power of Open Data'. Speech to the Locate 15 Conference, 11 March. Available from www.malcolmturnbull.com. au/media/speech-to-the-locate-15-conference-the-power-of-open-data

Yates, S. 2014. ANZSOG Data Sharing/Common Clients Roundtable, 20 November, Monash Law Centre, Melbourne.

Part 1: Governing in the information age towards better accountability

2

Shaping democratic outcomes in the information age

Paula Bennett

During my time as New Zealand's Minister of Local Government, Social Housing and State Services, as well as the Associate Minister of Finance and Tourism, I was interested in how we, the public service—and in that group I include myself—serve the public, the structures we have set up to do so and the data we use to inform our decisions.

Are we really servicing the public for their good? Or have we set up structures in such a way that it suits us as government, but does not reflect the types of lives people are living today, let alone in three or five years time? In my contribution to this volume, I wish to interrogate data analytics and the execution of that within our communities.

In my opinion, data is still largely locked inside servicing silos. We talk about silos frequently, but more important than just looking at it as a structure of the appropriation or the agency is realising that the available data is not being effectively used. Rather than applying it to real people's lives, streets and communities, too often the data is not shared as broadly as I think it should be. I personally feel a huge weight of responsibility. I should. I stand up and try to get re-elected every few years; I am in an incredibly privileged position to be able to instigate change and to work for the better of the people I serve. I genuinely feel that responsibility and I know that other officials do, too.

Similarly, when it comes to administering the kinds of services that people need, those officials responsible feel the weight of the responsibility to raise the standard to where it needs to be. We know so much about people's lives, but we have yet to work out how to use that knowledge and how to use that information as effectively as possible. In my opinion, what we lack is not *data* but *information* on what is happening on the ground, what is happening with people's lives and whether or not government spending is making a difference.

The focus of my chapter is social services, not simply because it is my background but because it represents two-thirds of New Zealand government spending. And if we are not prepared to constantly change the way we deliver services and constantly keep the changing needs of citizens in our minds, this fiscal challenge is only going to increase.

For me, it gets down to what the data actually tells us; the analytics, who to share it with and how. I think the public needs to give us permission to use data and anonymised data that is easy to understand—allowing us to go and say, for example, that there is a certain amount of children in a certain area with certain characteristics.

That is fine, and that can influence our policy decisions and our spending at a national level. But then you are faced with the question of how to use individualised data if you are to target the right kind of children and the right families. I think this is a challenge that we are yet to overcome. To this end, I have spent much of the last four years with my head in data analytics. I am passionate about the execution of this because, with all respect to them, a room full of pointy heads can sit around indefinitely pontificating on what data is relevant, how you merge it and what it actually means. I understand this because I too can get submerged in it and convince myself that it is the way forward.

This is all good and well, but we must then apply that data, I think, to execution: its value rests on what you use it for, how you use it for analysis and how you fast-fail and then build up what needs to be continued and scaled up. One recent example from New Zealand is a white paper on children. Considering we are a successful country full of opportunity, New Zealand suffers a terrible rate of child abuse, as does Australia.

It is to both countries' shame that there are children being seriously hurt and even killed in their own homes. This simply should not be. How do we tackle this? Some predictive modelling we did was instructive.

Over two years, our data analysts have gone through 200,000 cases, beginning in the mid-1990s, of New Zealand children who have been abused and neglected. Consequently, we can tell you about the 1,000 kids aged between six and nine that are most likely to end up in jail and/ or be seriously hurt or killed. What do we do with this knowledge? It is one thing to have the data and the information; it is quite another to then use it in line with your sense of responsibility. What I worked out was that we needed permission to use it, that it belonged to the New Zealand public. I also realised that all of New Zealand was in on the problem: when I stood up and gave speeches on child abuse, the usual response was that a quarter of the audience would cry and others would tell me that it was the most depressing speech they had ever heard. By contrast, when I would give a speech on welfare, everyone present would have an opinion. This was not true when it came to child abuse; I did not understand how to get that conversation going.

Our response to this problem was the white paper on children. In it we canvassed myriad ideas and we used predictive modelling. The question is, how do we generate interest and engage consultation in a subject that is so taboo; a subject that makes you feel physically ill?

One of the problems we face is that unless you have experience of abuse, it is hard to believe it is happening. And for those who are experiencing it, they are in such chaos and dysfunction that their ability to participate in any kind of process is zero. To combat this, I decided I had to use my political profile; in 2015, I led 32 meetings throughout the country. I purposefully did this in January when news is quiet and the media desperate for stories. This way, I figured, I could generate media and public interest.

We had a caravan travel the length of the country, talking to people and handing out postcards. We harnessed social media to canvass ideas, receiving thousands of submissions from a wide variety of people. In essence, we were asking middle New Zealand whether they were prepared for us to take money off them to spend on these kids; and whether they were prepared to allow us to gather information in order to determine key indicators and risk factors, allowing a more coherent approach to funding. Overwhelmingly, the people we spoke to wanted this to be done.

As a result of the information we have been gathering, we now know who has lived in a state house and who, generations ago, was under the mandate of Child Protection Services. We know who has been on welfare for generations. We know who was of interest to the police last week, who will be next week, and who has protection orders out against them. Additionally, we now have the infrastructure, in the form of an idealised system that overlays all of our ministries, to pull that data together. This then helps us decide what the key indicators are of where we are seeing failure and what we can do.

Gathering such data means nothing if you are not granted permission to use it. The stakes are high. One need only look to the UK's new child protection service, whose access to information was not handled well, setting them back, in my opinion, perhaps 10 years.

The UK example offers a salutary lesson of why this has to be carefully thought out, and why you need your citizens to understand what it means. In other words, they need a value proposition; you are appealing to a combination of hearts and heads. This is difficult, because we are asking the community to care for a group that they generally do not see and struggle to empathise with, given most New Zealanders live good lives. How do we get citizens to care about this demographic given they have their own worries, albeit less grave? If we genuinely care about others, we have to bring them with us. The public must understand that.

Open and transparent government is crucial. Sometimes I do not think we give the public enough credit for caring about the issues that affect society. In the age of social media, we think that policymakers have to be pithy to engage with the community or they will not be interested. This is false. They will if you engage them in a way that makes them believe they are part of a social contract; that we are all in this together, and that they need to do their bit. It is defeatist to assume that the public are not interested in complex issues, and to assume that you cannot engage them. In my opinion, if you cannot engage them, you have not tried hard enough.

The predictive modelling I have been involved in is a case in point. I would say to these people: 'What would you do if you knew?' 'What do you want me to do?' They had no idea. The general view was: 'Of course you should share information on our most vulnerable children. If you know that there is a history of abuse of the parents themselves, and that you have a custodial parent, of course you should share information'.

But one day I made the mistake of applying the key indicators to myself. I realised that 17-year-old me, on welfare, living in dismal conditions and living from one crisis to the next probably would have been in that box. Would I have liked my information shared? Would I have liked the prospect of social services were monitoring me and sharing my information with officials from health, education, the police and others? Frankly, it makes me feel squeamish even now.

I make this point to illustrate that it is all good and well when you are considering this information in regards to someone else. It is another matter entirely when it is about you, your family or your kids: suddenly you do not trust the government and they are the ones that hold the information and all of the power. In terms of gaining permission, the moment you do not give that due respect is the moment, in my view, the project fails.

Another thing we did was fundamentally change the whole welfare system by taking the power of politics out of the decisions of welfare. To do this, I introduced a multi-category appropriation (MCA), because too often politicians assume that because the public cares about youth, more money should be spent on youth—even though that might not be what the valuation and the data are telling you to be the most risky demographic.

In actual fact, what most of the data tells you is that it is those with low-level mental illness and the 50,000 people with back pain and obesity issues in our welfare system that need not be there if we had a different health response to them earlier. In this way, data can direct your spending. After introducing the MCA, I was told I was the first minister ever to give themselves less power. But with the use of data we have access to now, such a move was necessary.

And not only did we get voted back in but I ended up being the longest-serving welfare minister at that time. We did that by bringing the public with us while we drove a truck through fundamental system changes.

I would like to now move on to the issue of welfare valuation. With the help of Taylor Fry, an Australian firm, we applied an actuarial approach to everyone on New Zealand welfare. Why? Because having once been a single mother on welfare myself before finally landing a breakout job, I understand that what women in that position lack is confidence. They do not believe in themselves; they need to be asked what they want to do, and they need more backing when it comes to skills like writing CVs.

If we do this, spending a little more money at an early stage, we will get them off welfare. It's not the case that these women do not want to be off welfare—they just don't know how to get off it. Most of them have consistently been told they are rubbish; government has a responsibility to intervene early and set expectations higher for these women. All we need is a little more money at an earlier stage.

When I took this proposal to Treasury they were less than impressed, as was the Minister of Finance. I was told that we have increased spending over a sustained period of time only to see an increase in the number of welfare recipients. We are seeing, I was told, intergenerational welfare dependence at its highest, with more babies being born to women on welfare than ever before. If it was all about the money, they said, things would have changed by now. I realised I had to prove them wrong, which is why we did the valuation. Because ultimately what it did was give the statistics a level of openness and transparency that we had never seen before.

Thanks to this approach, we could see both where we were failing and where we were spending. It was easy. Armed with this information, we took all those people that were currently on welfare and figured out the characteristics of what we knew about them as a cohort. We then measured that over their lifetime and came up with a big number. The big number mattered because it got attention, but what really mattered was the micro information underneath the macro statistics.

We could literally look at the micro as far as cohorts, then break that up however we wanted, whether by region or by putting it in different characteristics, right down to the individual. We reached a point whereby, hopefully, any individual who walks through our door will know, at the tap of a keyboard, that their parents, for example, were on welfare for 50 years, that they have lived in public housing their entire life and that their risk factor for staying on welfare for a very long time is extremely high—making it worth us spending $30,000 in the next eight months to see if we can turn that around.

The first valuation of the total cost before the changes reported a NZ$78 billion liability; the next, after the changes, reduced that projection to NZ$69 billion. We saw real results as to what we were doing and whether it was working. This approach allows us to hone in on revealing details: 3.8 per cent of the drop between the two valuations, for example, was due to welfare reforms. That is the kind of detail we can get into. Granted, there are different factors to consider, such as the Consumer Price Index, but we can establish with confidence that 3.8 per cent of that $9 billion difference was due to welfare reforms. It is working. We are expecting more reductions, and we are on track for it.

I wish to now outline what we did with youth services in regards to data. According to conventional wisdom, the earlier you go on welfare the longer you are going to stay there and the higher the cost to the state. You think? But then we could literally break it down to *where*. To try to do this, then deputy prime minister Bill English thought, why don't we make it simple? We don't want them going on welfare. That is our outcome. Once we declared that to be our outcome, we decided that no longer could the government put kids on welfare. We just said no. Instead, we contracted with community youth organisations to set up a whole new system for kids who are not engaged in education, employment or training (NEET). We assigned our NEET kids a risk factor from low to very high, and we then put a monetary amount next to that risk factor because we did not want those youth services all skewing to the easier kids; we wanted to pay more for the more difficult cases.

We then told both the youth service and the kids themselves what outcomes we expected. And we rewarded the kids for the kind of behaviours we wanted. For example, once they have done six months in education, we give them an extra $10 a week, as we do once they have completed a budgeting course for six months. By this stage, we no longer give them cash, but instead pay their rent directly and put a small amount—no more than $50—onto a plastic card that they can spend. As for the youth services themselves, we pay them both an administration fee and a series of payments based on the milestones they achieve over a significant period of time. In this way, it is not just about the kids not going on welfare; it is about us making sure we reward positive behaviour to keep them off it.

This has now been running since 2012. In that time, we have seen a 21 per cent reduction in the number of young people going on welfare at the age of 19, a staggering drop. And yet, there are a few things we have not done that we should have, which is always the challenge of learning. While we may have collected really good data on *who*, what we did not do, but are now doing, is collect information on what the more successful organisations are doing. That said, in the space of three years we have managed to accomplish the lowest number of New Zealand's single parents on welfare since 1988.

We achieved that through data analytics: working out exactly who we are going to work with. We then individualised the data to avoid having to anonymise it, because we were doing it within the Ministry of Social Development's Work and Income. Looking at Work and Income, we had 300 women, all with similar characteristics; we decided to contract out 100, do intensive case management with 100 more and do nothing at all with the remaining 100. We then analysed the results at the 12-week mark, because that is how long it takes to get someone off welfare and into meaningful work. We could then evaluate the success or not and scale up what worked and stop what did not. It is that easy.

I wish to now turn to New Zealand's Better Public Services (BPS).[1] We have 10 of them, and they have changed the face of how government works. Although they encompass more than just social services, as State Services Minister I am responsible for all 10. As mentioned earlier, through this system we now have 38,000 fewer people on benefit. That equates to 42,000 children no longer growing up in a welfare-dependent home.

Collaboration is a challenge. The only way we will get more people off welfare, intervene in early childhood development and reduce crime is by engaging in cross-agency work. To that end, we are working on making it part of a chief executive's performance appraisal that they can demonstrably show that they have worked towards a BPS target that is not their responsibility.

Knowledge sharing is vital, and ongoing. One of the collaborative projects we tried to set up were the children's teams, an intensive group of professionals who are working with our most vulnerable. Interestingly, they shared *less* information when we put them together formally. They had been sharing information beforehand—with police, with social workers, with health professionals and with others—but once we put a formal structure around them, they questioned whether the sharing they had been doing was entirely above board. They actually stopped it, which is why execution is so important.

To that end, we now have an Approved Information Sharing Agreement in New Zealand, which we use often. Initially, this was an information-sharing agreement between government departments, but we have recently

---

1 Note that New Zealand's Better Public Services targets were refreshed on 3 May 2017: beehive. govt.nz/release/new-better-public-services-targets.

extended it to non-government organisations, sharing information internally. Should the next step be permission to share information from the people in question? I don't know. Should the parents of high-risk kids know that you see them as such and that you are going to spend more money on them? These are the sorts of things that we need to be debating: when it comes to the ethics of information sharing, we are better than we were, but we are far from perfect.

But how do we get departments to buy in, not just with their words but with their actions? To take that welfare valuation and welfare investment approach and build it across the whole social sector? This is the next challenge. And we have now worked out who we will focus on. We are going for that most vulnerable 15 per cent of the population. With the help of integrated data—which is where the data all sits—we have agreed on our key indicators.

These are for children: we are looking at the ages 0–5 or 12–24, and we are looking at the long-term benefit receipt. We consider whether an individual child has been at the attention of Child Protection Services, and find out whether they have a custodial parent and whether the child's mother has no education qualifications. Having two of those attributes is true for around 5 or 6 per cent of the population. To give you an indication, this means in a small city of New Zealand, where there are an average of 19,500 people aged 0–17, 477 of them have had a custodial parent at some stage, been at the attention of Child Protection Services *and* spent more than three-quarters of their life on welfare.

I have a few bottom lines. Basically, anything we do has to be positive for me to consider it a bottom line. The analytical techniques I have outlined in this chapter so far are one thing, but unless we fundamentally change how we work—what I call adaptive contracting—it means nothing to the children in question. In this way, if we do not spend as much time on execution as we are on the data analytics, we are doing a disservice to those 477 children.

Without help, these children have a dreadful future ahead of them. Essentially, unless we are succeeding at the execution stage, we will not be providing them with the kind of service they need. For me, execution has to be place-based. Why then has it not worked to the extent that it needs to? Quite simply, it is because politicians and senior bureaucrats tend to want to keep control. We are scared of failure, because we do not know how to manage risk and, when it comes down to it, we have not handed over the mandate and have not handed over the real money. I hope data analytics can be used to overcome our fears of mandate, accountability and risk with public money. We can genuinely use it.

Returning to those 477 children, people who understand data analytics recognise that if you know that there are a certain number of children in a certain place with certain characteristics, they display shared likely outcomes. Data analytics provides you with the indicators to measure success.

We need to stop telling these children what to do, and instead tell them what we want from them and clearly articulate how their success—or not—will be measured. Then give them all the flexibility in the world. By this, I mean looking at joint venture boards with real mandates and real money behind them, with a percentage of budgets that then measure success so they know exactly which children need help. Can we give them individual children's names? We are yet to work that one out.

To conclude, I would like to share a point that illustrates how serious we are about transparency in our next stage of work. One per cent of New Zealand five-year-olds are in families supported by benefits. If we look at an average group of 10 of those five-year-olds, they are high risk. Seven will not achieve education qualifications, four will go on to be on long-term welfare, and one-quarter will go to prison. In financial terms, each child in this group will cost taxpayers a minimum of NZ$320,000 over their lives, with some costing NZ$1 million. These figures are certainly attention-grabbing. Now the challenge is to execute a response.

3

Government as a platform

David Bartlett

Before being elected to the Tasmanian state parliament in 2002, I had been a chief information officer (CIO)—a kind of failed dot-com entrepreneur. This experience made me obsessed with finding new ways of having a conversation with my constituents using technology. I was sick of conventional community engagement conducted by backbenchers, in which constituents usually do not have a question per se, but rather a 15-minute incoherent ramble in their doorway.

That year, tapping into the stereotype that politicians are lazy and do nothing, I created a website that published my entire diary, enabling people to like things and friend me. What I have discovered subsequently, of course, is that I should have simply left politics then and created Facebook. Instead, this website was a monumental failure. I letterboxed my entire electorate and told them that if they had ever wondered what their local member does with their time, now they could find out and see my diary online.

Six months later, I discovered that really the only user was my mother, working out whether I was in her suburb and had come to visit her or not. And yet, fast forward six years, and I found myself premier of Tasmania, with 12,000 Facebook 'friends', all with the CapsLock key on, telling me what they thought of me, largely from the backdrop of anonymity.

It was these formative experiences that have led me to my current obsession: ubiquitous connectivity. The fact that we are all connected to our device of choice is massively disrupting the way we create wealth, changing the way we communicate with our customers(/stakeholders/clients/patients/students/constituents/ratepayers) and changing—in unexpected ways—the way we can solve old public policy problems.

There is a famous comparison of two photos, taken in the same place in the Vatican, eight years apart (Hill 2013). The first, depicting the 2005 election of Pope Benedict XVI shows a crowd of onlookers, one of which is filming the event on his Motorola flip phone. By contrast, in the photo of the 2013 election of Pope Francis, just about everyone in the crowd is capturing the event on their phone or tablet.

To me, ubiquitous connectivity is best described in images: the fact that—if you believe the Mobile Marketing Association of Asia (2010)—there are more people on the planet today that will put a mobile phone in their back pocket than people who will put a toothbrush in their mouth. All this in the reign of one pope. I believe it is the responsibility of government to learn—from citizens and from changing business models—new ways of creating wealth to better serve citizens in the way we co-construct solutions, both in service delivery and policymaking.

Last year, I took my children to Europe. It was the first time I had been to Europe as a tourist in 12 years. To plan that first trip, before my children were born, my future wife and I bought the Lonely Planet guide to Europe, a massive book. We physically cut out Estonia and a couple of other countries we were not visiting to save weight in the backpack. It was the tablet of stone that directed us where to eat, where to sleep, where to shop, what to see and how to get there. From a single voice, with a single point of view, in a single volume.

What did we do before the second trip? We used TripAdvisor. TripAdvisor is completely unlike Lonely Planet, that original tablet of stone. Instead of offering one view, it is a highly efficient marketplace, a platform upon which people like me who want information about travelling in Europe can share with others who have knowledge about tourism in Europe. We can get together and co-construct the solutions to my travel problems effectively.

In this chapter, I will argue that governments in Australia and New Zealand need to behave less like Lonely Planet and more like TripAdvisor. By this, I mean less policy handed down as tablets of stone and more co-construction, in which government provides the platform on which citizens, participants, experts and non-experts can co-contribute.

Throughout Europe, we used Uber, the online marketplace that connects people who have a car with those who want a ride. We used Airbnb, the online marketplace that connects people with a room with those on holiday. We found both platforms to be extremely efficient.

The recent platform disruption that has emerged in the commercial world has changed the way business models work. In addition, I believe it is disrupting the way government needs to work in the future. Consider the seemingly undisruptible model of selling pizzas: ringing up and ordering a delivery is perhaps the only innovation to occur in the pizza market for the last 40 years. But now, Domino's in Australia has created an app, 'Pizza Mogul', in which my 11-year-old son, Hudson, can construct his own pizzas. This not only allows Hudson to determine the service he gets from the pizza delivery shop, but also allows Hudson to develop his own pizzas and put them in the Domino's store for people to buy.

Every time someone buys one of Hudson's pizzas from Domino's, he is paid $1. In the year after releasing the Pizza Mogul app, Dominos Australia's share price rose by 41 per cent (Business News Australia 2015).

But what he has also done is create a marketplace in which people around Australia, including kids, can co-construct the product. He can sack all his pizza designers, and do away with market research, because, with the help of the app, the market is co-constructing the market research along the way. I will now analyse what is going on in the commercial sector, before exploring how we can apply this to government.

Essentially, since the industrial revolution there has been one business model to make a profit: you make a product, you sell it to customers, you do some sort of innovation (new price, new widgets, new colour, new flavour, new whatever), you repeat the process. Innovation might extend to market research.

But the emergence of the platforms I have earlier mentioned is disrupting this. The old way of wealth creation is being replaced by new models. Products are becoming services. In the pizza business, Domino's has created a much more personalised service than existed previously, but the really mature models are those in which services are becoming marketplaces. It is in those marketplaces, or platforms, that the value lies, because they engage the crowd—both experts and non-experts—in co-constructing the actual product. Think Uber, think Airbnb, think TripAdvisor, think Domino's Pizza.

In fact, the vast majority of the top 100 companies in Silicon Valley are those in platforms, not in services and products (Quantumrun 2017). The differing recent fortunes of TripAdvisor and Lonely Planet tell the story. In 2007, the BBC bought Lonely Planet for £130 million. In 2013, the BBC sold Lonely Planet for £50 million (BBC News 2013). That loss represents how much value has been stripped from the highly productised, single-voice model and distributed to the marketplace platform model.

If that much value has been stripped out of a commercial entity because of that the changing business model, how much value—whatever your meaning of that word—is being stripped out of government in its response to what citizens want?

In 2014, I gave a TEDx talk with the title, 'What the government can learn from the crowd', in which I argued that a digitally empowered and ubiquitously connected community is smarter than 1,000 policy wonks (Bartlett 2014). After the talk was posted online, I received a three-page dissertation from a friend, then the secretary of the Department of Premier and Cabinet in Tasmania, telling me why I was wrong. But I think he was wrong. My argument is that while there is a role for experts in government as a platform, there is a much more significant role for the non-expert population in co-creating solutions.

I will now outline some examples that illustrate how crowdsourcing can be both active and passive—and we need to think about both of these models.

Consider the following example. In 2008, when I was premier of Tasmania, the head of public health in the state, Dr Roscoe Taylor, warned me of the imminent threat of swine flu. He told me the virus was going to spread to Tasmania, and that consequently I needed to sign a cheque for $1 million to roll-out 32 swine flu clinics across the state where people in white coats will wait for the onslaught of swine flu–infected people to arrive.

It turns out the first strain of swine flu was reasonably innocuous. (This does not mean the second strain will be.) I asked Dr Taylor how we will know where the virus will spread and whether we could tactically deploy resources to respond to it. He said, we will not know.

Dr Taylor was wrong. Researchers at the University of Otago found that an accurate, advance predictor of where the virus was heading was people with a cough searching 'swine flu' in Google. By aggregating the data together and geolocating those searches, the researchers observed a nearly perfect 24-hour advance predictor of how swine flu spread from Mexico City to Australia, down to suburb, if not street, level. This is an example of passive crowdsourcing, enabled because of our ubiquitous connectivity.

A similar example occurred in the United States, when the City of Greater Boston decided to act on complaints about the state of its cycleways. Normally in this scenario a city would send out staff to locate the potholes and bumps, circle them with spray paint and a truck would come back to fix them. Instead, the city of Boston spent $5,000 creating a smart phone app that allows cyclists to record trouble spots. This has led to Boston being able to access a to-the-minute picture of every single bump or pothole in 3,500 kilometres of cycleways across the city. Not only do they have this, but they also have longitudinal study, because they are keeping the data over time to measure if those potholes and bumps are or improving or eroding.

I am a keen recreational fisherman. One thing that tells me climate change is having a big impact in Tasmania is that, as the waters off the island's east coast warm, I am catching fish species that I have never seen before. And I have been fishing Pirates Bay since I was a boy.

The app Redmap (Range Extension Database and Mapping project) allows me to log and geolocate a fish I catch. This, in turn, allows the CSIRO and the Institute for Marine and Antarctic Studies to tell me what the fish is, when it was last caught and how many others of its kind have been caught in the same area. These scientists have access to this data because across Tasmania, recreational fishermen like me are snapping their invasive species.

In other words, marine researchers have gained access to vast troves of data without having to send a boat out. And recreational fishermen get to have their catch recorded—an impact currency we like. This is another platform on which we are co-creating solutions to old and wicked public policy problems.

Through their use of technology, for the first time in history consumers are ahead of their major institutions—including government. Whether it be the Apple watch, the personal data measurer Fitbit or something else, the more people use technology, the more they expect it to shape their experience as citizens. And, traditionally, I think governments find that hard to deal with.

In 2013, bushfires swept through south-eastern Tasmania while flooding affected Queensland's Lockyer Valley, where my father lives; as my holiday shack was under threat from fire, my father's house was flooded for the third time in four years.

During those unfolding disasters, for the first time in history, I had access to better, richer and more accurate information from Twitter than I did from the traditional media. Within an hour of the fire front passing though, Mel Irons, a young woman 150 kilometres away in suburban Hobart, wondered how she could help those affected. She set up a Facebook page called 'Tassie Fires – We Can Help'. Within three days, there had been 35,000 interactions on this very simple Facebook page.

Now that I am no longer in government, if a light globe blows in my bathroom, I say to my wife, 'what's the government doing about that, anyway?' Because, of course, normally after a disaster like the 2013 Tasmanian bushfires, citizens turn directly to their government for help. Instead, in this instance, Facebook, a classic example of a new marketplace, was turned to. Thanks to Irons' page, whole flotillas of boats were organised to take supplies from Hobart to the Tasman Peninsula, cut off by fire.

When power went down in the fire-affected town of Dunalley, which is responsible for 70 per cent of the country's oyster spats, a plea for help was made on Facebook. Within an hour, six generators arrived to help save the oyster industry. This was a marketplace response that could never have been replicated by the old Lonely Planet approach. Only by the TripAdvisor approach.

I was surprised, two weeks after the fire, when the media reported claims that the government was doing nothing for citizens of the fire-affected area (Street 2013). I rang up my friend in the Tasmanian Department of Premier and Cabinet who was running the post-fire response and asked what was going on. There was a whole platform of people—a marketplace—

solving their own problems. Why was the Tasmanian Government not interacting with that? To this she replied that the Department of Premier and Cabinet had no Facebook policy.

By this time, Lara Giddings had succeeded me as premier, and she wanted to interact with this marketplace. What did she do? She wrote a press release with the Tasmanian Government letterhead and posted it on Facebook page, promptly attracting much online criticism.

Lara's mistake was that in engaging in these platforms, governments are no longer the experts. Actually, we need to create a platform on which experts and non-experts can co-create solutions in service and policy. We also need to recognise we are now a participant in that marketplace, which means sticking the Lonely Planet model on top of the TripAdvisor platform will not work. We have to be an authentic participant in the marketplace of co-construction, illustrated in the case of Finland outlined in Tanja Aitamurto's contribution to this volume (Chapter 11).

We see this in the commercial sector. The growth of investment in Silicon Valley and what the Americans call 'civic-tech' is massive. We in government need to move away from the old idea that when we want to consult the community on a particular issue, we set up a single website, provide information and invite. Instead, we need to embrace a much more citizen-centric approach of ubiquitous utility-like consultation; an engagement platform that is citizen-centric and that allows a citizen to say, 'I'm interested in forestry issues, I'm interested in legislation about off-road motor vehicles and I'm interested in neighbourhood issues in my area, tell me what's going on and I'll interact that way'. And that's the way we need to go. I should declare an interest here: I am a director of a Canadian company called Play Speak, founded by the former premier of British Columbia and former mayor of Vancouver, Mike Harcourt. He, too, recognised some of these problems post his premiership.

That is largely the end of my argument. Government faces many challenges in this space. The world used to be a roughly evenly divided triangle, with incumbents (think the existing invention of pizza) at the base, innovators (half Aussie, half Hawaiian–flavoured pizza) in the middle, and regulators (the marketplace in which pizza is sold) at the top.

But in today's world, the innovators, pushed by the consumers armed with their mobile devices, are stretching that triangle out in favour of platform wealth creation. Think of the following triangle to illustrate this: incumbents (the taxi industry); regulators (department of roads and transport) and innovators (Uber). The consumers and the workers are massively driving these changes. But we have not in government, I think, adequately sought to understand this new regulatory environment, let alone the environment in which we need to be the innovators in government, service delivery and policy.

References

Bartlett, D. 2014. 'What the Government Can Learn from the Crowd: David Bartlett at TEDxHobart'. 18 January, *YouTube*. Available from www.youtube.com/watch?v=POz3xBaCA9c

BBC News. 2013. 'BBC Worldwide sells Lonely Planet business at £80m loss'. 19 March, *BBC News*. Available from www.bbc.com/news/entertainment-arts-21841479

Business News Australia. 2015. 'Innovation Helps Drive Domino's Profit to $64M'. 11 August. Available from www.businessnewsaus.com.au/articles/innovation-helps-drive-domino-s-profit-to--64m.html

Hill, D.J. 2013. 'Before/After Of Pope Announcement Shows Incredible Proliferation Of Mobile In Just 8 Years'. 14 March, *SingularityHub*. Available from singularityhub.com/2013/03/14/beforeafter-comparison-of-pope-announcement-shows-incredible-proliferation-of-mobile-in-just-8-years/#sm.00043scct1e4gdz1tsu1wwc0c0an8

Mobile Marketing Association of Asia. 2010. 'Industry Leaders Discussed Possibilities of More Consumer Centric Mobile Marketing Campaigns'. 19 April. Available from www.mmaglobal.com/news/industry-leaders-discussed-possibilities-more-consumer-centric-mobile-marketing-campaigns

Quantumrun. 2017. '2017 Quantumrun Silicon Valley 100'. Available from www.quantumrun.com/company-ranking/2017/2017-quantumrun-silicon-valley-100

Street, J. 2013. 'Fire Victims Feeling "Overlooked"'. 29 January, *ABC News*. Available from www.abc.net.au/news/2013-01-29/fire-victims-feel-27overlooked27/4488742

4

Are we there yet? Government online: Lessons from New Zealand

Colin MacDonald

In terms of governance, the New Zealand environment is quite different, of course, to Australia's: we have the pleasure of only having two layers of government—central and local. We have just over 30 central government departments, and 78 local government authorities. New Zealand has 4 million people—and a widespread diaspora of 1 million overseas. One of the things that is really important to our current government, and therefore to all of the public service, is the delivery of better public services. This is one of the government's four priorities, along with responsibly managing finances, building a more productive and competitive economy and supporting the Christchurch rebuild after the 2011 earthquake.

We at the Department of Internal Affairs New Zealand have the responsibility of leading one of the results embedded in the delivery of better public services, which is Result 10,[1] aimed at making it easy for citizens to transact in a digital environment. But, interestingly, the department is also the home of a role called the government chief digital officer, occupied by me. It's one of three functional leadership roles in

---

1   Since 2012, a group of 10 agencies, in an initiative known as 'Result 10', have been given a mandate to radically change the way government delivers services. Working collaboratively to develop joined-up, integrated life-event products and services across government, enabled through digital and secure options, the aim is that by 2021, 80 per cent of the most common transactions with government will be completed digitally.

our government and entails my trying to work across silos: interesting and challenging for anyone who's tried to do that because all of our accountability models go up to ministers and yet services to citizens go across the silos. This is one of the key themes of this volume: citizen-centricity.

I think it's a huge opportunity. Because, for me, when I think about the problem, the challenge, the opportunity of digitising government, sometimes I can become quite daunted. There's a lot to be done. There's a lot of ways we can change and do things differently. I think the prize is absolutely enormous. And as public service leaders, we have a phenomenal opportunity to make a real shift in the way citizens experience government. (By 'public sector leaders', I don't simply mean 'public administrators'—if we think of ourselves solely as administrators we might as well all go home because digitising government needs real leadership. It is administrative leadership rather than political leadership but it needs leadership nonetheless.)

My contention is that the traditional government service models are no longer fit for purpose. They do not even come close to meeting what citizens are experiencing in other parts of their lives; we are a long way from 'Amazon-like' government.[2] If it was truly an Amazon-like government experience, it would be completely different to what it is today. It would be much easier for the customer. We would be connecting the dots behind the scenes. We would not be waiting until somebody applied—for example, we would be proactively offering people the opportunity to get their entitlements.

It would be faster. It would be more efficient and we would be doing quite a different job. But how? To be frank, I'm not quite sure. That may be a terrible admission coming from the chief executive of a government department, but I don't know how to achieve this, other than having a clear vision and taking it one step at a time. Importantly, we actually have to get started doing things. We are working in what is effectively an organic system. It is too complex to be knowable. Intervention logic does not work here.

---

2   Amazon doesn't ask customers to deal with its packing website and then its shipment site, but governments still ask citizens to navigate their internal bureaucracy. In an Amazon-like government, this bureaucracy still exists, but is behind the scenes of the citizen experience.

We have to try things, we have to disrupt the status quo and we have to see what happens. We have to then respond to that change to the system. It is quite a different thing and it is quite hard, I think, for us to do an Amazon level of experimentation, given the pressure on us from politicians and the public. Instead, I think we need some golden rules.

First, put the customer at the centre. This is of course easy to say and incredibly difficult to do because citizens are individuals: they have unique needs, expectations and contexts that we won't always know. There are broadly two types of customers we need to think about: those to whom we deliver services; and those we regulate. Because, after all, we are still regulators. The time may come when we truly have an Uber experience where we are all regulating each other; but, until that happens, government still has a role to set the rules and to try and help society work in a sensible way.

To this end, in New Zealand we have put a lot of effort into trying to understand customer needs, divided into stages. Stage one has been about identifying some customer personas, to act as ways of helping people to think about the different types of customers they might be dealing with. Much work has gone into trying to say that, broadly speaking, there are these types of citizens who have these types of characteristics.

But while this gets us started on the journey, it is still only a proxy for actual customer experience. And yet, when I think about where we are and where we are trying to get to, it's not a bad start. For example, in New Zealand we have over 500 government websites. We stopped counting once we reached 500. And that's just for our central government. All of the sites have a different look and feel, they have different approaches, but most of them cannot actually complete your transactions online. To take this next step forward, we have produced a new website, www.govt.nz.

We were inspired and helped by colleagues in the UK. They gave us all of their source codes and we went through an alpha and a beta test and we launched the website. But within six weeks, despite all this hard work, we had changed it dramatically. This isn't to say I am critical of the process. We did exactly the right thing, particularly at the point when the team came back to me and said they wanted to make a significant change to the look and feel of the site, even though it had only been running for six weeks. It was exactly the right thing to do because, while the initial site was nice and easy for people to use and to find information, it didn't feel authoritative; it didn't feel like government.

Consequently, we tweaked it. We changed the typeface, we changed the colours to make it look a little sterner. We learnt this lesson: in our effort to become user-centric, we created such a different experience for users that they didn't trust it to the level that we wanted them to.

Part of putting government at the centre in the digital world is to make sure we can really easily figure out that the person at the other end of the bitstream is who they say they are. In New Zealand, to do this, we have a product called Real Me. It started off as a purely government product, but we have now partnered with New Zealand Post, a state-owned enterprise, to deliver it into the private sector as a product that they might want to use in their digital world. The reason we've done that is because we realise that people transact infrequently with government. And there are three things that this authentication product can do.

The first thing it can do is let you log on to a service. The second thing allows you to verify your identity. But, importantly, the third thing it enables is allowing you to exchange information in a way that you can control and manage. To borrow an example given by Tamati Shepherd elsewhere in this volume (Chapter 13), in the future when you change your address online, all of the agencies to whom you've given permission will be able to receive that address change. If you don't have the identity piece solved, in my view, getting the digital piece solved will simply not happen. And I know in the UK they have taken a different approach to this, using the private sector to figure out the authentication problem. I'm not convinced that this is something that we can leave to the private sector. While there is much the private sector can do, I'm not sure that deferring to them the level of authority to confirm that somebody is who they say they are is what we in government want. Time will tell if that's a wise decision.

My second golden rule is to design services around life events. People don't get up in the morning and think, 'I'd really like to get in touch with the Department of Internal Affairs today, they're nice folks, we'll have a nice chat'. They tend to give us a ring when they want to go overseas, for example, they want to get their passport. It's not so much that they want to get their passport; they want to travel. So we've put a lot of energy into making it really easy to get your passport.

New Zealand is the only country in the world where you can apply for and have your passport approved online. It is then posted to you, typically in three or four days. It is a world-leading service. We are not going to put much more money into it because it's a standalone service. The next step to improve it will be to find ways of integrating it into people's lives—perhaps on the Air New Zealand website. When you try to book your flight, for example, should you not have a valid travel document, you could apply via the airline website. Because that would be a much more sensible way of doing it.

We are currently identifying a whole range of life events with which we can integrate our services. The first one is the birth of a child event. When your child is born, instead of having to then go and register with multiple departments, ideally, you would be able to do this via an app. New parents are busy. Using such an app would be much easier than having to go to wherever the relevant government office may be when you've just had a baby.

This is an example of why figuring out design around life events is crucial. It is also hugely challenging, because we can't simply stay within our own organisational silos. In fact, I believe this is the most fundamental challenge to our current operating model in terms of government. This will be a very big issue to solve and, if we don't do it, it will eventually trip us up.

To avoid this scenario, we have to work differently. We can no longer work as a simple service provider or a government department. We have to work within a system of services. This is the third golden rule. To this end, in New Zealand, we are trying to take a hybrid approach. We describe it as being centrally led but collaboratively delivered. There is no way that I can see somebody at the centre orchestrating all of this. And yet, somebody does have to take a leadership role and try and help others by guiding the way. That is effectively my role, to try and provide that overall guidance while chief executives remain accountable for delivery within their own organisations.

Fortunately, the state services commissioner has now put an expectation on all chief executives that, along with me, they will take a leadership role. They must play fairly and join in: it's a question of trying to balance agency and system priorities.

Neither of my first three golden rules have anything to do with technology. The fourth one does. We will have to transform information and communications technology (ICT) to succeed. We have built our systems and our methods and our ICT shops individually and separately. What we need to do instead is start driving an ICT ecosystem that actually does work together. In New Zealand, a lot of energy over the last couple of years has also been put into the backend of all of this, the stuff that a few of us get very excited about.

I get excited about it. I have been playing in the computer science space for a long time. This topic interests me because I know how much payback you can get. And so we have done a lot of work trying to encourage agencies to take ICT as a service offering rather than continue to invest in their own infrastructure. Not just because it saves money, but because when we come to start looking at how we exchange information, how we create end-to-end business processes, if they're all being built on consistent platforms, those business processes will work together much better. The information flows will be much more straightforward.

It also gives us an opportunity to build stronger security across the ecosystem because, at the end of the day, all of this needs increased public trust and confidence. There is a fundamental difference, in my view, between trust in public and private institutions. If citizens lose trust in government, they don't have a choice—they cannot simply say 'to hell with that, I shall get my passport from somebody else'. They can try, but it would be a bad idea because in doing so they would be breaking the law.

Compare this to the private sector. If I have a bad experience with ANZ—who I used to work for so I feel I can name them—I can simply take my business elsewhere. I have a choice. Citizens do not have a choice about who they can draw services from. Therefore, service quality and efficiency becomes one of the pillars that underpins trust and is part of the fundamental relationship between the citizen and the government. In turn, it is incredibly important that we maintain that trust. But we lose their trust if we don't transform the services to look more like the services that citizens experience in the rest of their lives. If we do this badly and we breach privacy, we will lose trust. If we don't do it, we will lose trust. Our only choice is to do it well and gain and maintain trust.

To reiterate, only one of the four golden rules is about technology. Most of the challenges are actually about how we tackle this problem. And, in my view, we are reinventing the way citizens interact with government, and there isn't the same level of risk tolerance as there is in the private sector, there is a different level. But I do actually echo the points that we have to try things but we also have to create an environment where we are trusted to try things. That requires an interesting conversation with ministers. How many of your ministers have said, 'go on out there and fail'? 'Go and get us on the front page of the newspaper for that service failure, that will be a good thing.'

We all know what that is like. We have all been there, one way or another. The wonderful thing about the private sector is you can bury your mistakes. You can actually refuse to give information about your failures. The private sector can do this. We as public servants cannot. Unfortunately, that means the risk is much greater for us, but in my opinion, if we don't make those aforementioned changes, we will lose citizen trust. Consequently, we must tackle some big rocks.

I think one of the big rocks is the service or operating model across government. As agencies, each of us is currently providing our own service; each of us thinking about the customer as a customer of our agency. We have to figure out a way to break that mindset, and instead start thinking about people as citizens of the government, customers of the government. We have to figure out how to manage these trade-offs between the system approach and the agency approach.

This isn't easy. When you've got a minister screaming in your ear saying they want benefit payment done on time and they don't care about whole of government, and you've got another minister in your other ear saying they want the experience of government to be changed, we are the ones caught in the middle. But it is our job to take leadership of that and find the way through. It is not a political issue. Politicians consider it to be public service business, so we simply have to get on with it.

For me, the big challenge in all of this is governance and accountability. What do public servants do when they are not sure what to do? You've heard it before: we set up committees. This is what we have done. We have set up one called the ICT Strategic Leadership Group. I'm not usually proud of committees, but I am of this one. Because in this case, I have managed to secure the time and the energy of 10 of my chief executive colleagues to sit on that ICT Strategic Leadership Group.

Here's the secret of its success. This isn't really about ICT. This is about transforming government. Consequently, of the groups that report to this and are guided by this committee, only one of them concerns technology. The other three are about much more interesting and important things like the service innovation, the service experience, the sharing and management of information, the mining of information, the use of information to drive better outcomes for citizens, and figuring out how the funding models and any revenue models have to change in order to support this approach. Because, as earlier stated, our old models won't support us.

We have managed to make progress but, I can tell you, some of the stuff that has been hardest has been getting our public management approach to fit a cross-horizontal, sectoral method. Within those groups, we have got more than 50 senior leaders. These are involved chief executives or second-tier leaders, from 19 central government agencies. The cynical amongst them might think it's just me trying to spread the blame if things go wrong, but I firmly believe it is time to spread leadership and get more people on this journey.

Earlier in this chapter, I mentioned funding as being one of the big challenges, and one of the learnings for me in this area is to follow the money. If you can figure out how to follow the money (or ideally, lead the money), this will get much easier. And one of the things I think we have to do next is look at how we approve investment in agency-based transformations. I know that Singapore is doing interesting work in this area, involving a balance between an agency investment and a system investment. I think we need to move that way as well.

But, in the end, it's all about the benefits. For me, this means trust and confidence. It all comes back to that. If we get that right then citizens will start to consider government to be an effective and an efficient partner. And it will start to talk to issues such as the lack of engagement between citizens and government (fewer people voting, fewer people getting involved). Technology is not the answer, but it is one of the tools we can deploy within this change in experience.

To return to the question: are we there yet? In his contribution to this volume I think Tamati Shepherd was right when he mused that if we think we are then we are probably on the wrong journey. No, we're not there yet. We have taken some steps. We are making some progress. As an example, the Result 10 target is that, by 2021, 80 per cent of New Zealanders' most common transactions will be online. In 2015, the figure was 46 per cent. That continues to be a challenging target. As for Real Me, we have got 62 log-in services delivered through 20 agencies. We have more than 2 million accounts, driving millions of log-ins. We have 60,000 verified accounts, with that number growing rapidly.

Real Me is a quality product; it won the security and online safety award in the 2014 Australasian internet awards, and was a finalist in the UN public service awards in 2015.

Moreover, we are starting to deliver services around life events, although it is early days. There are two aspects to this: sharing *for* the customer, which is reusing their information and making it much easier for them to be able to do what they want to do; and sharing *with* the customer, in a privacy-protected way, providing information to service providers that those people may want to use.

Although I have not mentioned the private sector much in this chapter, my final point is that it has a huge role to play. Whether we talk about it as an Amazon-style system or something else, the idea of government as an ecosystem requires the creation of an environment whereby the private sector can come in and provide services that citizens can then choose to use.

And yet, we will have to set the rules. We will have to be what's called the ecosystem driver—if you talk to Amazon, that's what they did. Amazon drove that ecosystem. They decided where it was going to go, they decided what the rules were and they then attracted people towards them. As governments, not only do I think we can do that, I think we must do it. We need to drive the ecosystem. We need to make it not just okay for the private sector to play; we need to make it positively attractive because we cannot provide all the service needs that our citizens are going to be looking for in the future.

5

Trans-Tasman perspectives on transparency in decision-making: A view from Australia

Anne Tiernan

It is widely asserted that Australia's political culture is broken: that we have lost the capacity for long-term thinking, and are unwilling and unable to embrace necessary reform. In his contribution to this volume, Oliver Hartwich (Chapter 6) points out that Paul Kelly and other members of the Australian media share this view, and contrast current experience with a generally more successful past. Australians, I think, increasingly look to New Zealand for its more successful recent record of innovation and reform. How did it come to this? We have long since become accustomed to being outperformed on the rugby field, but that it has extended to governance has made us all uneasy.

My contribution to this volume is informed by two ANZSOG-funded research projects: one on prime ministers' chiefs of staff (Rhodes and Tiernan 2014), and one on examining the dynamics of central executives in four Westminster-style countries—Australia, Canada, New Zealand and the UK (Rhodes and Tiernan forthcoming). We have also developed cases from Queensland and Victoria to provide a subnational and a federal comparison.

These projects provide a unique contemporary insight into the working dynamics of decision and advisory systems—those networks at the very centre of government. They also highlight some themes that are relevant, I think, to this volume's focus on transparency and engagement. The primacy of coping and survival in the calculus of political administrative elites, for example, cannot be overstated and is evident in all four countries. While efforts to address fragmentation and project coherence across policy and politics are ubiquitous, this seems to be a quest with neither end nor likely success. The current trend across all types of political systems is a push to centralisation and small group decision-making. This is creating myriad problems.

Comparisons between Australia and New Zealand often claim that reform is easier to undertake in New Zealand because it is not a federal system. I am very heartened that Oliver Hartwich did not claim this in his chapter. We should acknowledge that the unitary parliament, mixed-member proportional (MMP) electoral system of New Zealand places a powerful constraint on executive leaders in Wellington. I am persuaded that the MMP has an impact on political culture. I am less persuaded by the federalism argument. A lack of checks and balances has, at times, for example, led New Zealand to implement some horrible policies, particularly in housing regulation and others.

But I do think former prime minister John Key was an extremely interesting case study. Moreover, I think trade exposure and a much more existential experience of economic uncertainty has focused New Zealanders' minds on reform in a way that the mining boom maybe insulated Australians from doing. And yet, I think there is something generational about John Key and his deputy (later prime minister) Bill English that I think is very interesting. I would have put former NSW premier Mike Baird in the same category. And maybe in New Zealand it is an issue of scale, but I think there is also an interesting point to be made about that country in regards to career politics.

I suggest that the broken political culture—seen prominently in its difficulty to enact reform—is it least partly the result of structural problems. They are embedded in, and an unintended consequence of, successive waves of reform and change within the Australian core executive over the past 40 years. And I argue that ministers—particularly prime ministers—have driven many of those changes but, taken together, those actions and decisions have undermined both the quality of advice and support that is available to them (in terms of routines and processes that provided advice and options), and the opportunities to consider it, debate and contest it.

Lest anyone think I am verballing any particular leader, I would note that questions about the performance of prime minsters' and premiers' offices have featured in the reviews into the defeats of the Napthine and Newman governments, both one-term governments; and the challenge to Tony Abbott's leadership in February 2015 and September of that year, when he eventually lost it. The same was true of Kevin Rudd and Julia Gillard, as Rod and I explore at length in our books.

It is not accidental, I think, that we are seeing profound loss of trust in the capacity and integrity of our political processes and institutions. One need only consider the social media response to revelations Bronwyn Bishop took a tax payer–funded helicopter flight from Melbourne to Geelong—since dubbed 'Choppergate'. This sentiment is also evident in opinion polling and, I think, quite starkly in the recent defeat of two first-term governments in Victoria and Queensland. And yet, it seems, politicians do not learn.

This is a real challenge, and I think there is a structural reason why it is happening. I also think it is significant that in August 2015, two Australian national newspapers (*The Australian* and *The Australian Financial Review*) hosted a National Reform Summit that specifically excluded politicians. Such engagement across sectors sent the message that organisers felt there was no point having the political parties at the table, since neither would engage in serious debate about reform. Perversely, leaders respond to that kind of pressure and complexity by turning inwards. They retreat to ever-diminishing circles of close advisers and supporters.

Of course, it is extremely difficult to get on the front foot. Nobody knows that better than me, having spent much time around ministers and prime ministers. But being informed and prepared about the dynamics of leadership—the constraints and contingencies as well the opportunities—can, I think, help immensely.

You do not achieve that by systematically undermining the institutional memory and your capacity to learn from experience in the systems of advice that support decision-making. Because of this, we can see the limits of centralisation and the lack of openness and transparency often associated with it. Problems are constantly exposed through the lack of coordination and coherence across the ministry and government—take 'captain's picks', a new term that has entered the political lexicon. Poor communication and sequencing of decisions compound the situation, as does a cabinet process whereby major issues are introduced 'under the line' only to be leaked, creating policy reversals in the face of apparently unexpected resistance. That is simply bad process and poor governance practice.

How have we ended up in this situation? I think there are fundamental questions to ask. Transparency is important but, for me, we are reaching a point where capacity and effectiveness have become the key questions. And yet, leaders seem either unable or unwilling to recognise them— or they are so locked in their own path dependencies that they cannot recognise the underlying structural cause of their difficulties is them.

My chapter will focus on the impediments to reform and change that I think are inherent to the hybrid advisory system it has developed. New Zealand is nowhere near as far down this path as is Australia. Australia is at one kind of extreme. Queensland's a little further along that spectrum of hybridisation and expectations of political responsiveness; Victoria is somewhat less so. And then we have New Zealand and the UK at the other end. Our fieldwork revealed that Canada had shifted much more towards the hybrid model than I had expected.

What then are the impediments to reform and change? I have identified three: the loss of institutional memory; the associated failure to learn from experience; and leaders' lack of organisational capacity.

I will now outline some potential reform directions, noting that they featured in the difficulties experienced by current and former prime ministers and premiers. I argue there are lessons to be learned from New Zealand, but I think too much of the debate in Australia is focused on the performance of the public service and not enough on the demand side of the relationship.

Overcoming some of the problems that I have raised would require the political class to both reform and change its modus operandi and be prepared to embrace arrangements and frameworks that support rather than undermine their capacity to set and maintain a focus on priorities. This also applies to their ability to control the political and policy agenda within the constraints of what you can do in a very unpredictable environment and their ability to negotiate and manage the many relationships, contingencies and dependencies that characterise life at the centre of government. They really do not seem to have understood how much the context has changed.

Readers would be aware that everywhere, leaders are reshaping their advisory systems to cope with common pressures. We have seen growth, institutionalisation, hybridisation and politicisation (a contested term, but in this context I mean the advent of partisan advisers). There is a blurring of the boundaries between partisan and non-partisan sources of advice. There has also been a significant growth in centralisation around leaders, as anybody who works in Commonwealth or state government will be able to tell you. Communication and issues management are becoming predominant, and bureaucratic routines of control and coordination are struggling to cope with system demands.

Recent Australian prime ministers, going back to the election of John Howard in 1996, have struggled to make a successful transition to the office. Howard, Rudd, Gillard and Abbott all faced trouble. Rudd was arguably more successful in his transition in the first 12 months, mostly because of the support of the leadership team, with John Faulkner playing an especially important role in as special minister of state. It is often forgotten that John Howard himself faced leadership speculation in 1997 after the travel rorts affair.

Remember that? There was something to be learnt from that, I would think. But Howard was never challenged for the prime ministership, the reason being that he subsequently learned lessons and made changes to deal with the difficulties and criticisms that he faced. The other three faced leadership challenges early in their terms. It has been an unprecedented period of leadership instability.

The problems leaders have in navigating the transition to office are often attributed to the pace and complexity of decision-making. This has been well described. But the recurrence of this under four successive prime ministers, and a number of premiers, means we need to ask ourselves further questions.

The work with chiefs of staff and the project I am currently undertaking has revealed significant concerns about institutional memory within the central executive. The problem is well understood in the presidential context but less so at the level of political leadership in Australia, where it is acute at both the state and Commonwealth levels. I have already outlined some of the drivers, but I think the major point to consider is that institutional memory is essential to the ability to learn from and avoid repeating the mistakes of your predecessors. That 'Choppergate' occurred on the same side of politics so damaged by the travel rorts affair of 1997 starkly illustrates how little has been learned.

Really, then, the problem of a lack of institutional memory is one of leaders' own making. It is a relatively recent development, and even if they may not be conscious of it, they are largely responsible for it. The decision to shift their main source of advice and support from the Department of Prime Minister and Cabinet and the Department of Premier and Cabinet into the prime minister's and premier's offices, respectively, has had profound consequences. In effect, the prime minister's office is now performing key coordinating tasks that were once the province of the public service, making the role of the chief of staff especially critical. And yet, most recent appointees to this role have had very little bureaucratic experience and very few networks on which to draw when they come into the job.

As we demonstrate in the book, the pathway into the job today differs from the way it was in the past. As does the way out: when central figures of the prime minister's office leave, the whole show must start over. I had a lot of trouble persuading my co-author Rod Rhodes that this was the case. He found it absolutely unbelievable. But, over time, we were able to empirically demonstrate that this was, in fact, so.

I think another problem is the contemporary hyper-partisanship of Australian politics and the consequential reflex to denigrate and smash the legacy of the people who you have just defeated. The dilemma here is that a new government spends its first two years in office dismantling their predecessor's agenda before they enact their own. I think this limits and inhibits the ability and willingness to learn.

There is no doubt that the hybrid advisory model that has evolved in Australia since the 1970s has given ministers greater responsiveness and political control. But it has not resolved the fundamental questions of competence and responsiveness. Ministers remain dependent on many things, including the public service. Therefore, the need to preserve institutional memory remains important. New Zealand does a much better job of preserving institutional memory in a systemic manner.

The hybrid model has made it the responsibility of prime ministers to organise and manage the advisory system, instead of leaving that to people who know how to do it.

It has put a burden on political leaders they did not have before. I don't believe they have particular insight into that. One of the striking things revealed in our research everywhere, with the possible exception of New Zealand, has been an increasingly distant relationship with the public service. The centre of the central executive no longer regards the public service as central or even necessary to decision-making. From the public service's perspective, this makes just 'keeping in the loop' difficult, let alone adapting to the dilemmas this changing context provides, in terms of the ability to influence it.

And yet we still talk about public sector reform. There is, of course, the question of the contestability of more fluid advisory systems. But while it is good to have alternative sources of advice (and ministers think this is very important), there is a fundamental problem of institutional memory with ad hoc arrangements. Evert Lindquist (1999, 2007) has done some work on this in the past. It raises questions about where authority lies.

Organisational capacity is a concept drawn from the presidential studies literature (Burke 2000, 2009; Dickinson 1997; Dickinson and Lebo 2007; Greenstein 2004). In the American context, where you have a whole bunch of people moving out and a whole bunch of new people moving in to take over with each change in presidency, they really have to think about how they are going to operate the machinery of government. In Australia, until recently, we have not needed to think about such things. The public service provided administrative continuity to support changes of government.

In the Australian context, organisational capacity might include things like forging an effective team; recruiting an appropriately qualified chief of staff; making sure good people serve in the prime minister's or premier's office. It also requires being able to coordinate; work with others; develop effective relationships (across the ministry, say, or the party room); ensure quality advice is coming in; discipline the flow of advice and create effective arrangements; communicate the narrative; and try to coordinate what we all know is a very difficult set of arrangements to coordinate. But there are still many disciplines you can bring to bear; it's just that a career in politics doesn't necessarily prepare prime ministers to do that.

Nor, frankly, do I think having to focus on such things is a very good use of their time or expertise. We need to have a different conversation with political leaders.

So what might be done? There is no going back to the model as it was before, despite the lamentations of some. This is because politicians won't allow it, but also because staffers do things that public servants shouldn't and can't do. However, I am interested in the reform agenda as being much more to do with what could be done to preserve institutional memory. I have some specific suggestions regarding this.

What we know is that there has been persistent resistance from Australian politicians—not just to reforming travel entitlements but also (on both sides) to attempts to become the focus for reform and change themselves. Sir Arthur Tange talked about this in the 1980s (Edwards 2006). It is very interesting. Leaders need to be persuaded that they are poorly served by their current arrangements and, for me, this is the next frontier. I am struck by the New Zealand experience on this: they have got responsiveness, but it is still heavily predicated on the role of the public service. This does not mean the public service has a monopoly or policy advice, or that ministers do not seek alternative points of view. But they are doing it in a way that still maintains a degree of institutional memory.

In this context, I was feeling a little depressed about how things are going in Australia. And yet, New Zealand is not above critique. Their ministers' critiques of public service advice is that it is not sufficiently citizen-informed. But whatever their frustrations, New Zealand ministers do seem to accept that the public service is important in terms of continuity and institutional memory.

To conclude, when it comes to transparency, what I think we really need to think about is how all these mechanics work at the centre of government. Currently, we know surprisingly little about it. The empirical work that has been done in this area is by myself and Rod Rhodes, and it's an area that needs further research. In other words, there is really no institutional memory to operate the very central parts of government. That is a frailty that worries me. I think we need to be debating this much more seriously; I think ministers need to stop being the elephant in the room of public sector reform and become part of it.

References

Burke, J.P. 2000. *The Institutional Presidency*. 2nd edition. Baltimore: Johns Hopkins Press.

Burke, J.P. 2009. 'Organizational Structure and Presidential Decision-Making'. In G.C. Edwards and W.G. Howell (eds), *The Oxford Handbook of the American Presidency*. New York: Oxford University Press, pp. 501–27.

Dickinson, M.J. 1997. *Bitter Harvest: FDR, Presidential Power and the Growth of the Presidential Branch*. Cambridge: Cambridge University Press.

Dickinson, M.J. and M. Lebo. 2007. 'Re-examining the Growth of the Institutional Presidency: 1940–2000'. *The Journal of Politics* 69(1): 206–19.

Edwards, P. 2006. *Arthur Tange: Last of the Mandarins*. Sydney: Allen & Unwin.

Greenstein, F. 2004. *The Presidential Difference: Leadership Style from FDR to George W. Bush*. Second Edition. Princeton: Princeton University Press.

Lindquist, E. 1999. 'Reconceiving the Center: Leadership, Strategic Review and Coherence in Public Sector Reform'. Organisation for Economic Co-operation and Development. Available from www.oecd. org/officialdocuments/publicdisplaydocumentpdf/?cote=PUMA/ SGF(99)5&docLanguage=En

Lindquist, E. 2007. 'Organizing for Policy Implementation: The Emergence and Role of Implementation Units in Policy Design and Oversight'. *Journal of Comparative Policy Analysis: Research and Practice* 8(4): 311–24. doi.org/10.1080/13876980600970864

Rhodes, R. and A. Tiernan. 2014. *The Gatekeepers: Lessons from Prime Ministers' Chiefs of Staff*. Melbourne: Melbourne University Press.

Rhodes, R. and A. Tiernan. forthcoming. *Ministers and their Courts: Evaluating Ministerial Support Systems*.

Rhodes, R., J. Wanna and P. Weller. 2009. *Comparing Westminster*. Oxford: Oxford University Press.

6

Trans-Tasman perspectives on transparency in decision-making: A view from New Zealand

Oliver Hartwich

Transparency can mean many different things. It could mean, for example, that some things can never be fully transparent: no matter how much we wish for transparency in government services, some areas of government policy simply do not open themselves to that. Intelligence, the police and secret services are obvious examples, but there are other cases involving commercial and sensitive information; trade negotiations, as with the Trans-Pacific Partnership, is one. Some areas of government policy will probably never be as transparent as we would like them to be.

In my contribution to this volume, I wish to explore the link between transparency and the political reform process. When we are talking about the policy process, we are interested in how to make it predictable, interactive and open—in short, how transparent we can make it. I would argue that the question of how transparent we can make government processes in policy formulation is closely linked to the ability of the government to reform.

You might call this the reform responsiveness of government or the reform ability of a country. Transparency, I think, is the key to getting a government on the path of reform. I explored this in some detail in the essay 'The Quiet Achievers', published in 2014 by the Menzies Research Centre in Canberra (Hartwich 2014).

As well as offering trans-Tasman perspectives, this chapter will also include observations from Germany, where I am from, and the UK, where I have worked. I now live in New Zealand, after having worked in Australia. Looking at these different countries, what you can see is that the way in which government policies were introduced, how they were prepared and how transparent they were ultimately determined the outcomes and long-term success of these government policies.

First, some background. In 2014, New Zealand returned prime minister John Key for a third term. At the time, what I found interesting was the markedly different ways in which the Australian and New Zealand media covered this event.

The Australian media typically presented the story as being a radical, reformist, neoliberal government being returned to power—something they saw as surprising, given the prevailing narrative in Australia was that reform was a thing of the past and no longer possible. Paul Kelly has been writing variations on this theme in his column for *The Australian* for many years. His consistent message is a rather bitter and predictable contrast of the 'end of certainty' when reforms happened (of which Kelly was chronicler), with today's sobering experience of watching nothing much happen (see, for example, Kelly 2013, 2014a, 2014b).

Whether it was Henry Ergas (2014) writing in *The Australian*, or Peter Hartcher (2014) in the *Sydney Morning Herald*, the Australian media consensus was that John Key was a massively reformist, ambitious, activist prime minister implementing his agenda and being returned as a reward. Contrast this with the New Zealand media's take on the event. Neither the *National Business Review* (Hosking 2014) nor the *New Zealand Herald* (Edwards 2014) were describing John Key in these terms.

This was the starting point for writing my essay 'The Quiet Achievers': I wanted to determine which set of commentators was best describing the approach of John Key's government. The essay also came in the context of Australia's reform holiday; arguably the last real, decent micro-economic reform enacted in this country was the introduction of the Goods and

Services Tax (GST) in July 2000. And even that was not nearly as good as the New Zealand one. The contrasting commentaries also came in the context of a general mood that reform is something that is no longer possible, a view held by Paul Kelly but also President of the European Commission Jean-Claude Juncker, whose famous dictum is that we all know what needs to be done, we just don't know how to get re-elected once we've done it (*The Telegraph* 2014).

Finally, the essay was written in the context of an increasingly positive story about New Zealand in the Australian media. Just three years earlier, I had to explain my decision to move from Australia to New Zealand; I was swimming against the tide, the annual migration loss from the other direction at the time was 40,000 people, a massive figure for a country the size of New Zealand.

But the narrative has changed. By late 2014, the Australian media wondered in awe at how a country that had not only lived through the global financial crisis (GFC) as Australia had—except without the aid of a mining boom—and then done battle with a few earthquakes was still closer to a budget surplus at the time than Australia was. Who was right? Was the Key Government a reformist government, or was it was really just as hopeless and dithering as Rodney Hide (2014) wrote in the *National Business Review*?

My essay's basic conclusion was that the Key Government was what I call one of incremental radicalism. In the Key Government, we saw a government that does quite a few radical things, but it did them step-by-step, one bit at a time.

Consequently, if you gave Key long enough, he probably would have reformed the country substantially—just not in one fell swoop. I determined to identify the strategy behind Key's approach. Because I once studied marketing, I came up with a snappy formula. It is an analogy to the 'four Ps' of marketing: place, price, promotion and product. In Key's case, I thought it was rather preparation, patience, pragmatism and principles. If you want to add a few more Ps, maybe you could add passion and performance; for now, I think the four Ps will do.

Fundamentally, my essay was trying to explain how Key, his former deputy (and eventual successor) Bill English and the whole New Zealand Government have significantly reformed the country in a way that does not alienate huge parts of the population and allows them to get re-elected.

I think it largely comes down to transparency. Because what the Key Government did very successfully was establish narratives. It established these narratives by explaining what it was doing, how they were doing it and why they were doing it. They consulted; they took time. Let me explain this further through the four Ps of the Key Government.

The first P is preparation. Preparation means it takes a significant amount of time before anything really happens. That preparation time is necessary to build the narrative, to take the public along the journey and explain why what they are doing is necessary. In her chapter in this volume, Paula Bennett (Chapter 2) admitted how long it took until the government actually figured out what they were trying to achieve and how they were going to do it. Paula Bennett herself is perhaps the best example of this preparation approach: she spent the Key Government's first full term laying the ground for the welfare reforms that the Key Government would introduce in the second term; she basically spent three years preparing with the welfare working group, consulting widely.

Proceeding from this preparation P is the patience P. I think it is a mistake for governments, especially newly elected governments, to try to do everything at once and introduce all policies in one single budget—a mistake Tony Abbott made in 2014. Key would not have done that. He took a very long-term approach to introducing his policies. This approach requires patience, but patience is required to do the preparation properly and to consult widely. Key consulted widely, not just with special bodies like the welfare reform working group but also with organisations like the Productivity Commission, a relatively new organisation in New Zealand, having been introduced in Key's first term.

With patience comes pragmatism. No matter how much Fairfax columnist Peter Hartcher (2014) described John Key as a neoliberal activist, first and foremost I think he was a pragmatist, because he knew exactly what he could get implemented and what he could find majorities for. He would not go far beyond that and he would never wait for the opportunity to introduce a first-best solution that might never arrive if he could, at least, get a second or sometimes a third-best solution in place, then start work on refining these second- and third-best solutions.

So far these three Ps of preparation, patience and pragmatism could also describe Angela Merkel. But there is a fourth P: principles. With Angela Merkel, you never quite know where you land: a former Social Democrat

Defence Minister in Merkel's first cabinet once said that if Merkel was the pilot of a plane, her passengers could board the flight in the knowledge that they would arrive safely, as long as they did not care where they land (Hartwich 2015). This is because Merkel basically makes up her policies on the go—on the fly. She commissioned 600 opinion polls in her second term, which *Spiegel* magazine revealed in 2014; an average of about three a week. *Spiegel* called it 'government by numbers', and that is not far off (Huggler 2014).

Merkel basically takes any kind of position and its opposite. She has been chancellor for over 10 years and I still have no idea what she really believes in. I think with John Key, we saw a very different kind of politician. I think we could all tell where his instincts lay, even though he did not implement everything in one go. It was clear John Key wanted to lead New Zealand towards a more market-based approach, an approach that incorporated micro-economic reforms, but ones that were introduced gradually with carefully laid groundwork.

This was the rough picture of the Key Government: one that was driven by preparation, patience, pragmatism and principles. Typically, as long as he stuck to his four Ps, it worked well for him: for his personal approval ratings, for his party and for the country as a whole. Deviating from the four Ps did not work so well for him. With this in mind, I will now provide a few examples of both successes of the Key Government and what I consider to be some of the failings. I will then explore the limitations of the four Ps.

First, on fiscal policy we can see the approach of the four Ps worked quite well. A chapter of my essay is called 'The Patient English', referring, of course, to Key's Minister of Finance (and successor as prime minister), Bill English. English was an incredibly patient finance minister, never losing sight of his ultimate goal of leading the budget back to surplus. But he did it, I think, in a way that was both incremental and successful in difficult circumstances; we should not forget the Canterbury earthquakes of 2010 and 2011 cost the public sector massively. The second example where I think reform worked remarkably well was Paula Bennett's welfare reforms, an investment approach she pioneered and the subject of her chapter in this volume.

The counterexamples where the Key Government failed to deliver were those instances where they did not spend enough time preparing, nor have the patience to explain what they were doing. A prime example, I think, was education minister Hekia Parata's attempt to reduce class sizes in spite of overwhelming research indicating good teachers are more important than small classes. She wanted to just change the priorities of her department's spending, but she did not explain why she was doing it. Her plan was introduced without much consultation and so it completely backfired on her.

The other example, I think, are social impact bonds, a policy introduced by the Key Government in 2015, on the Queen's Birthday holiday weekend. Bizarrely, the government picked mental health as the area for the first social bond. For a relatively experimental policy, I think this was not the right approach. Rather, they should have first explained why they were doing it. Very few people had ever heard of social impact bonds—they are still a relatively new instrument internationally—and the one area in which they have worked best, and where there is the most experience internationally, is in reducing recidivism among criminals.

I think the government could have done a much better job at explaining what they were trying to achieve, pointing towards international examples and taking the public with them on this new policy instrument of social impact bonds. Instead, they went straight into mental health, one of the most controversial areas. It backfired on them.

The other limitation to the four Ps approach and to radical incrementalism, I think, is public opinion. John Key was very well aware of public opinion—probably as much as Angela Merkel is—and therefore there are some issues that, because they would be unpopular, he simply would not have tried to prepare the public for changes to, even if they were necessary. One example that comes to mind is foreign investments regulation. Another example is radical changes to local government finance and the housing market. In this sphere, I think Key was probably too timid to go beyond what was achievable, even in the medium term.

I would like to now make a point about the role of the media in New Zealand's reform process. I do not think there is a big difference between the Australian and New Zealand media in this regard; there are not many columnists and journalists in New Zealand making the case for reforms.

Instead, we unfortunately see a very stereotypical left-versus-right debate when instead the New Zealand media should be debating what works and what doesn't in a more empirical way.

In any case, let us return to the question of transparency. I think what we can learn from Key's example is the importance of transparency. Because if you communicate your policies well, if you establish a narrative, you have a much better chance not just of implementing them, but ensuring they are not changed at the next government, let alone at the next opinion poll. With that in mind, I think John Key did a relatively good job as prime minister. He was not a perfect prime minister by any measure; he was certainly not a perfect politician (not that I believe either exist). And yet, Key got many things done while still keeping his personal popularity high and retaining the public's support.

I wish to now mention some international counterexamples of what happens when you do *not* take this approach. One of the prime examples that comes to my mind is the German Government of Gerhard Schroder, who led a centre-left coalition of the Social Democrats and the Greens. In the winter of 2002/03, with unemployment at more than 5 million, Schroder introduced massive welfare reforms—but not nearly as radical as those Paula Bennett introduced in New Zealand. The difference between Paula Bennett and Gerhard Schroder was that Schroder spent no time whatsoever explaining why he was doing it. All he basically said was, 'we've got 5 million unemployed, we have to do something'. But he did not establish a narrative around it. Paula Bennett, in contrast, established a narrative of needing to help people. She basically said, 'we have a national crisis and we need to do something quickly'.

Without such a narrative, Schroder was punished. He was punished personally, with his approval ratings going down. His party was punished and they are yet to recover. When Schroder first became chancellor, the Social Democrats typically received around 40 per cent of the vote; they have been in the ghetto of around 23–25 per cent since his welfare reforms. These reforms were undoubtedly necessary, but never communicated well.

Another example, I think, is David Cameron in the UK. In opposition, David Cameron hardly ever talked about the issues he then had to tackle as prime minister. He hated talking about Europe. I know that because I worked in David Cameron's favourite think tank, and we were not allowed to use the E-word because it was so divisive for the Tory Party.

Cameron never wanted to talk about it, which was traumatic for his own party. He knew precisely what happened to his predecessors so he did not spend much time on it in opposition.

Nor did he talk about austerity, nor alternatives to Labour's spending programs—until in 2010, he was prime minister and suddenly had to do something about the economy and the budget deficit. Likewise, once in office, under pressure from his own backbench, UKIP (the UK Independence Party) and circumstances, he suddenly had to talk about Europe. That approach is not how you win public support for instituting reforms. Yes, he won the 2015 general election, but in fact there has never been a UK Government re-elected on such a slim popular share of the vote as Cameron's. He did not do particularly well at introducing these reforms.

As a final international example of how not to institute reforms, I think I am fair in stating that Tony Abbott did not adequately communicate what he was trying to do in the 2014 Budget. He certainly did not take the public with him. This is in contrast to John Key's New Zealand, where you saw a government attempting to be as transparent as it could in explaining its case for reform and trying to take the public with them. I think this approach is the only chance we have in today's society to introduce reforms that are necessary, and which some commentators believe are no longer possible, at least in the Australian case.

To conclude, I believe New Zealand should encourage us all that reforms are still possible, as well as demonstrating that to be successful, reforms need a good marketing plan, a good strategy and a good narrative.

References

Edwards, B. 2014. 'The Next Three Years of National Boredom'. 22 October, *New Zealand Herald*. Available from www.nzherald.co.nz/ opinion/news/article.cfm?c_id=466&objectid=11346602

Ergas, H. 2014. 'There's Much Tony Abbott Could Learn from John Key's Triumph in NZ'. 22 September, *The Australian*. Available from www.theaustralian.com.au/opinion/columnists/theres-much-tony-abbott-could-learnfrom-john-keys-triumph-in-nz/story-fn7078da-1227065791798

Foley, C. 2014. 'Victorious New Zealand PM Pledges More of the Same, Eyes 4th Term'. 21 September, *Yahoo News*. Available from www.yahoo.com/news/polls-open-zealand-election-212405219.html

Hartcher, P. 2014. 'Team Key Teaches Lessons on Democracy to Team Australia'. 23 September, *Sydney Morning Herald*. Available from www.smh.com.au/comment/team-key-teaches-lessons-on-democracy-to-team-australia-20140922-10kgv3.html

Hartwich, O. 2014. 'Quiet Achievers: The New Zealand Path to Reform'. *The R. G. Menzies Essays No. 1*. Ballarat: Connor Court Publishing. Available from www.menziesrc.org/images/Publications/Quiet_Achievers-the_New_Zealand_Path_to_Reform.pdf

Hartwich, O. 2015. 'Under Merkel, Germany is Asleep at the Wheel'. 6 August, T*he Australian*. Available from www.theaustralian.com.au/business/business-spectator/under-merkel-germany-is-asleep-at-the-wheel/news-story/f212fd3db1b5bcc30a91ddd9f90dd1db

Hide, R. 2014. 'Flag Debate is Next Poll Distraction'. 11 October, *National Business Review*. Available from www.nbr.co.nz/article/flag-debate-next-poll-distraction-bd-163619

Hosking, R. 2014. 'The Meaning of Election 2014'. 26 September, *The National Business Review*.

Huggler, J. 2014. 'Angela Merkel Commissions "More than 600 Secret Opinion Polls"'. 9 September, *The Telegraph*. Available from www.telegraph.co.uk/news/worldnews/europe/germany/11082171/Angela-Merkel-commissions-more-than-600-secret-opinion-polls.html

Kelly, P. 2013. 'Australia Votes Yes for Competent Government'. 9 September, *The Australian*. Available from www.theaustralian.com.au/opinion/editorials/australia-votesyes-for-competent-government/story-e6frg71x-1226714801300

Kelly, P. 2014a. 'Politics in Crisis and a Nation in Denial'. 2 July, *The Australian*, p. 16.

Kelly, P. 2014b. *Triumph and Demise: The Broken Promise of a Labor Generation*. Melbourne: Melbourne University Press.

The Telegraph. 2014. 'Jean-Claude Juncker's Most Outrageous Political Quotations'. 15 July. Available from www.telegraph.co.uk/news/worldnews/europe/eu/10967168/Jean-Claude-Junckers-most-outrageous-political-quotations.html

7

Did community consultation cruel climate change?

Ron Ben-David

By way of introduction, 2006 was not a particularly exceptional year in history. No empires collapsed. There were no memorable assassinations. We were spared political scandal of any note. It was the year, however, that Twitter was launched and Pluto was demoted to a dwarf planet. It was also the year that Cyclone Larry devastated a large swathe of the Queensland coast only months after Hurricane Katrina wreaked havoc in New Orleans and the Gulf of Mexico. In my part of the world, Melbourne, 2006 was the year it stopped raining. In Melbourne, the level of our water storages became a topic for daily discussion on the nightly news and in the print media; the *Age* ran a countdown clock—the number of days until Melbourne ran out of water, the number of days until Doomsday.

In October 2006, an unassuming official in Her Majesty's Treasury published a lengthy report into the economic effects of climate change (Stern 2007). Until that time, climate change—or 'global warming', as it was then known—was viewed as a fringe issue for greenies only. Nicholas Stern's report changed all that. Seemingly overnight, climate change moved from the greenstream into the mainstream. In Australia, the unfolding drought supercharged the shift in public attitudes towards climate change. It was some time either very late in 2006 or early in 2007 that I started hearing chatter of the possibility of state governments commissioning an Australian Stern Report. The chatter quickly dissipated.

Then, out of the blue, on 30 April, the then leader of the federal opposition Kevin Rudd and the premier of Queensland Anna Bligh announced on behalf of the states and territories that Professor Ross Garnaut had been commissioned to conduct a review into the economic and policy implications of climate change for Australia (Garnaut 2008a). Consider that for a moment: this review by the states and territories was announced by the leader of the federal opposition. I am unaware if this arrangement has any precedent in the history of the Australian Federation but it was certainly very unusual.

Within hours of the announcement, I found myself appointed to head the review's secretariat. It was to be one of the great privileges of my public service career to work with Ross and our incredibly dedicated team. It was an 18-month adventure that consumed us completely and in which we delighted. In my early discussions with Ross, a few principles quickly emerged about how we would conduct the review. It would be a very open process of enquiry intended to engage the community as broadly as possible. We would take nothing for granted and nothing as given. Instead, we would scrutinise and test every fact, assumption, assertion and idea that was presented to us, and we agreed to an approach where there would be no surprises: any conclusions that we were to reach would first be disclosed fully and tested publicly.

I have no idea how many discussions, meetings and public forums we held around the country, but it must have run into the hundreds. Likewise, I can't remember how many papers we released or how many speeches Ross delivered during the review. But we used every occasion possible to air publicly our findings and thoughts.

On 21 February 2008, Ross delivered an interim report to premiers and chief ministers and the new Rudd Labor Government in Canberra. A subsequent meeting of the premiers and chief ministers in Adelaide provided the perfect opportunity for him to hand over the report formally. Our communications manager insisted Ross hold a press conference after the official event. Sitting in the airport lounge en route back to Adelaide, I watched it on Sky News. I was awestruck. Something extraordinary was taking place in front of my eyes. The interim report was being given blanket coverage. Discussion of the report and the response of commentators continued largely uninterrupted all afternoon. This was followed by days of ongoing coverage and discussion in the electronic and print media. In all fairness, while the report was good, it was only very preliminary in its thinking and in its analysis.

What was going on? Why was the level of interest so intense? No doubt, it had something to do with Ross Garnaut's personal standing in the community and the media, given his long and distinguished role in modern Australian public policy. But I believe something else was going on. It was as though, finally, intelligent and open debate about climate change had been legitimised. The release of this pent-up demand for discussion, debate and analysis was to create a bow wave that was to last for the remainder of the Garnaut Review and take the public policy discussion to its high-water mark.

The month that followed that day in Adelaide could be described as *La Belle Époque*, a golden age of discussion, reflection and debate on all matters associated with climate change. However, I do not want to over-romanticise the times. There were heated disagreements, and sometimes these were not pretty, but they were conducted in the open. And that is the unique feature of *La Belle Époque*. Everything was on the table for all to see. I am very proud of the role the review played in promoting that wonderful, though ultimately fleeting, moment in the public policy discussion about climate change. But even as we were being swept along by this extraordinary tide, countercurrents were forming.

Shortly after the release of the interim report—by which I mean a few hours after the release of the report—the then Minister for Climate Change, Penny Wong, held a doorstop press conference (see Murphy 2008). She told the media that while the government welcomed the interim report as an important input, it would also be looking to other inputs. This comment came to be known, with some degree of infamy as the 'just one input' statement. Was the minister's comment intended with disrespect or malice? I strongly doubt it. What the minister said was self-evidently true. Governments do not and should never outsource policy decisions. Nevertheless, the timing of her comment and the context in which it was delivered enlivened all the vested interests who were threatened by the openness of our approach.

I will return to this matter shortly. But just to complete this little tale: some months later, Ross appeared at the National Press Club (Garnaut 2008b). When asked how he felt about being 'just one input' into the government's thinking, he responded, 'I'm just one input into the prime minister's thinking and he is just one input into mine'. The next few months were a whirlwind of intellectual enquiry, consultation, production and sleeplessness. Rather than share that full, long story, I will dedicate the rest of this chapter to explaining why, despite our best efforts, the community soon became so disaffected with the issues, how climate change moved from the high-water mark of public engagement reached during *La Belle Époque* to its near antisocial status today. I will propose four contributing factors. No doubt there are others.

First, in the Garnaut Review, we sought to make the case for action on the grounds of rational analysis using scientific and economic methods of enquiry; in modern lingo, we were committed to 'evidence-based policy'. At the same time as we were embarking on that endeavour, others sought to impress upon the community that the need for action was a moral imperative. Indeed, even the prime minister framed it as 'the greatest moral challenge of our time' (Shanahan 2007). Framing the issue in such terms certainly appeals to those who already agree—and those who already disagree will just ignore or dismiss such claims. But what does it say to the people who are not well versed in the issues, members of the community who are yet to form a view, who do not yet understand the claimed need for action?

In the words of George W. Bush, I think it says to them you are either with us or against us. Such a political message may work in the US, but I suspect it has the opposite effect in Australia. Morality is based on belief and I suspect Australians don't appreciate being told what to believe. There is another important aspect of this political involvement in the public discourse worth mentioning. Typically, when governments commission independent enquiries, in whatever form they take, the political echelon tends to withdraw from the public discussion, leaving the review to run its course and leaving the politics until later. Precisely the opposite occurred during our work. For reasons I will shortly reveal, throughout this period, the government was constantly discussing the issue in the media.

The second factor that I believe eventually eroded our efforts to engage and involve the community were the competing processes established by the newly elected government. During the preceding election campaign, the then Rudd opposition committed to establishing an emissions trading scheme within 18 months of being elected. I will not comment on the merits of that commitment, but what it meant was that the newly established Department of Climate Change was immediately tasked with designing and implementing the promised scheme.

That was a herculean task and I greatly admire the department's efforts. However, it meant that alongside our work, which was focused on understanding climate change and identifying the appropriate policy response, the department was running a parallel process into designing the policy response that had already been announced during the election campaign. Now, couple the department's parallel process with the minister's comment about the Garnaut Review being just one input into the policymaking process, and what happens? I suggest that it invites— no, it almost begs—all the vested interests to shop around and play off one process against another. And, to be clear, I am not just referring to the brown interests of the coal or aluminium industries.

Green interest groups, such as those advocating renewable energy and energy efficiency, were just as active in pursuing their agendas. What was perhaps the worst consequence of these coincidental reviews was that they reopened doors that had temporarily been shut to the whisperers. Our attempts to flush all the issues into the open and put them squarely in the public domain, to expose them to the sterilising effects of public scrutiny, those efforts were being thwarted as doors in Canberra were again open to those who wanted to come in and have a quiet chat. As a consequence, some of the vociferous public debate on the day of Ross Garnaut's press conference had begun to dissipate. More worryingly, some of it simply disappeared from public view altogether.

The third factor I would like to highlight was the battle over language or, more specifically, the battle over how and in what terms the public debate over climate change was to be conducted. There's nothing new about such battles. They occur every day on mostly every important issue. As the Canadian public intellectual Marshall McLuhan observed half a century ago, he or she who masters the medium, masters the message (Whitman 1981). I suppose we too tried to influence the medium in which we believed the climate change discussion needed to be conducted. We used what we believed was the language of analysis and scientific method. We did not shy away from admitting that we could not be certain about all the facts, nor did we demur from admitting that, in such instances, we could only rely on our best judgement about how to proceed—and those judgement calls were exposed for all to see and for all to question. One example of our attempts to establish reasonableness as the medium for discussion related to how we assessed the evidence about climate change itself. In the review, we stated:

> The Review takes as its starting point, on the balance of probabilities and not as a matter of belief, the majority opinion of the Australian and international scientific communities. There are many uncertainties around the mean expectations from the science with the possibility of outcomes that are either more benign or catastrophic. (Garnaut 2008a, Chapter 2)

Admittedly, that is not the sexiest of prose. But its central message—that we do not have all the answers so the best we can do is look at the available evidence and we must do so as analytically and as rationally as we can—surely that must be the most obvious message of all. What chance did this gossamer-like message stand in moderating the medium when, at the same time, ministers were making public speeches declaring river systems will die before our eyes, we have overloaded the Earth's atmosphere, the Earth's gifts are not guaranteed, nations may disappear? And so the climate change discourse quickly degenerated to one in which people would be challenging each other with the question: do you believe in climate change? How truly inane!

Do we stand around asking each other whether we believe in quantum mechanics, even though we cannot see it with our own eyes? Do we feel compelled to profess our faith in magnetic resonance tomography before submitting ourselves to an MRI scan? We lost the battle over the medium. The medium became marked by the language of certainty and absolute commitment and, in doing so, it also became the language of exclusion and division. The language of certainty, commitment and exclusion became the medium, a medium in which there was no room or need for open engagement and genuine enquiry. For me, perhaps the tackiest example of attempting to control the medium was the name given to the proposed emissions trading scheme in 2008.

It was to be called 'The Carbon Pollution Reduction Scheme'. Pollution? No one in the scientific community refers to carbon dioxide as a pollutant, but such details didn't matter in the battle for control of the medium. By branding it a pollutant, someone was seeking to ensure they controlled what we thought about it and what we thought about anyone who might dare to not yet agree with us. Cynicism begets cynicism, and when such cynicism imbues the medium—well, is it any wonder the community turned its back on climate change as an issue worthy of national discussion?

The fourth reason for why we moved from the height of community engagement with the issue of climate change in early 2008 to the nadir that followed is much simpler than the other three reasons. Quite simply, the drought broke. We're all human. If, over a few years, we are filled with images of parched landscapes while, at the same time, we are bombarded from the *zeitgeist* about messages about climate change, then those two things become associated in our conception of the issues. When one ends, we cannot help but feel somehow the other is also lessened.

I have provided four reasons that I believe set the stage, even as early as 2008, for the retreat of the community from the issue of climate change. First, despite our efforts to build a case for action from first principles in evidence, we could not stop others from asserting—indeed, imposing— climate change action as a matter of moral imperative rather than rational consideration. Second, despite our efforts to bring into the public spotlight all the issues and all the competing interests, we found ourselves competing with other processes that soon gave those interests avenues to retreat from the spotlight. Third, despite our efforts to establish a medium of engagement and enquiry, the language of certainty, commitment and exclusion soon became the medium. And fourth, the drought broke.

Looking at these four explanations, I admit it appears I am casting blame for the demise of climate change policy on everyone and everything but the Garnaut Review. Rest assured, I am too burdened with self-doubt to let myself get away with that. In the years since the review, as I have reflected and pondered about the role the review might have made in the unfortunate saga of climate change policy. I have repeatedly asked myself: Were we right to build the case for action from first principles and evidence? Were we right to try to bring all the issues and all the competing interests into the public spotlight? Were we right in our efforts to create a medium of engagement and enquiry for discussing the policy issues? Over and over again, I keep returning to the same three answers. Yes. Yes. And yes. We were right in trying to do all these things. I expect that most readers would agree with me. Indeed, I expect that most of us would view these three endeavours as being self-evidently right. They would seem to embody the most fundamental principles for any public enquiry, indeed, for any serious discussion of public policy.

But here is my problem. How do we know? How do we really know that these are desirable endeavours for reviews and discussions of public policy? Maybe we don't really know. Maybe we just believe them to be true. Maybe we are confusing belief for knowledge because, for most of us, these objectives are somewhat self-serving. They fit neatly within a romantic notion of selfless public service. But has it been proven? Can it be proven that public involvement in policy formation is self-evidently desirable? And, if it be true, then is it always true? Or just sometimes true? If it only be sometimes true, then who gets to decide? And outside of us few, as well as those with a special interest, who really cares about what they decide? In the end, might public consultation really just be a sop to the vanity of the privileged few? I hope not.

Rather than conclude this chapter deep in existential angst, I will share with you one final tale from the Garnaut Climate Change Review, a tale that may help shed light on yet another consequence of extensive public consultation. As I have recounted, throughout the review we sought to make our thinking known publicly so that there would be no surprises at the end. We consulted and consulted and then we consulted some more, so much so that, by the time of the final report, we already had said pretty much everything we had to say. We succeeded so mightily in avoiding surprises that, when the review's final report was released, the news services struggled to find anything to report. Eventually, they did find something.

It lay in a table on page 542 of the report; a table on page 542 became *the* story. In passing, that table listed a study estimating the emissions reductions that would be gained from swapping beef for kangaroo meat. That became the news story. Page 542 even made the international news services with Bloomberg's report appearing under the headline: 'Skippy on the menu as Australia seeks to fight global warming' (Heath 2008). And you can still go to the website, it's still there, and there are the pictures that they've got accompanying the story. And that was it. After 18 months of exhaustion and exhilaration in equal measure, our efforts had come down to that headline. It was a surreal end to a very real endeavour, an endeavour that sought to engage fully the community in the development of public policy.

References

Garnaut, R. 2008a. *The Garnaut Climate Change Review—Final Report*. Commonwealth of Australia, Cambridge University Press, Melbourne. Available from www.garnautreview.org.au/index.htm

Garnaut, R. 2008b. National Press Club Address—Launch of Supplementary Draft Report: Targets and Trajectories'. 5 September, Transcript. Available from www.garnautreview.org.au/CA25734E001 6A131/WebObj/Transcript-NationalPressClub-5September2008/ $File/Transcript%20-%20National%20Press%20Club%20-%205 %20September%202008.pdf

Heath, M. 2008. 'Skippy on the Menu as Australia Seeks to Fight Global Warming'. 16 October, *Bloomberg*. Available from www.sott.net/ article/167594-Skippy-on-the-Menu-as-Australia-Seeks-to-Fight-Global-Warming

Murphy, K. 2008. 'Unless change is in the air, Australia could become… The Biggest Loser'. 22 February, *The Age*.

Shanahan, D. 2007. 'It's Monty Burns vs the Whippersnapper'. 30 April, *The Australian*. Available from www.theaustralian.com.au/opinion/ columnists/its-monty-burns-vs-the-whippersnapper/news-story/f82 c521b6fa5deb1131cfd8664fe38cf?sv=a08348e114e849126f2854 c6a9fe4cc1

Stern, N.H. 2007. *The Economics of Climate Change: The Stern Review*. Cambridge, UK: Cambridge University Press. Available from www.webcitation.org/5nCeyEYJr?url=http://www.hm-treasury.gov. uk/sternreview_index.htm

Whitman, A. 1981. 'Marshall McLuhan, Author, Dies; Declared "Medium Is the Message"'. 1 January, *The New York Times*. Available from archive.nytimes.com/www.nytimes.com/books/97/11/02/home/ mcluhan-obit.html

Part 2: Building trust through civic engagement

8

Transparency, trust and public value

E. Allan Lind

My chapter concerns trust in government, a topic that has attracted considerable attention recently. I write from the perspective of an academic social psychologist, but one who has been involved in government and policy studies for many years. About 40 years ago, I began working for the US federal government—this was during the Carter administration; I worked for the research arm of the judicial branch—and as I look back, I am struck by how much better the technology of government is now than it was then. I am not thinking of electronic technology, but rather how much better we are now at using knowledge and research methods from the economic and social sciences to design and evaluate policy options.

Nowadays, we are often quite sophisticated in our research on the impact of policies and in our understanding of the social terrain that we are working with as we create and execute government initiatives. At the same time, though, there is a troubling trend with respect to at least one aspect of how well government works. Improvements in the science of government notwithstanding, people do not seem to think their governments work in their interest. Data compiled in recent years by the Organisation for Economic Co-operation and Development (OECD) show that, on average, public trust in government is decreasing. Figure 1 shows the percentage of poll respondents who said they trusted their national government. The graphs show the average trust ratings in 2007 and 2012 for all of the countries included in the OECD data set, and they show the nation-specific percentages for Australia, New Zealand and the United States. The results general show a reduction in trust. New Zealand seems to have 'dodged the bullet' of erosion of public trust, but clearly in Australia and the United States something disturbing is happening.

Figure 1: Percentage of poll respondents who trust their national government
Source: After OECD (2013).

The OECD data was collected across a five-year period, but the same trend is seen in longer-term comparisons, which show that in many countries, citizens' trust in government has been decreasing over the last several decades. This is a matter of concern for those of us who would like to think that government is an effective *and* valued realm of human endeavour. Disturbing, too, is the fact that it is trust in *national* government that is taking the biggest hit—Figure 2 shows the OECD trust averages for several societal institutions (in 2012). Trust in national government is lower than trust in the judicial system, local police, the education system and healthcare. (The data for the individual nations included in Figure 1 all show similar patterns of relative trust in these five institutions, again with the exception of New Zealand, where trust in the national government was slightly higher than trust in the judicial system, though lower than trust in the other three institutions.)

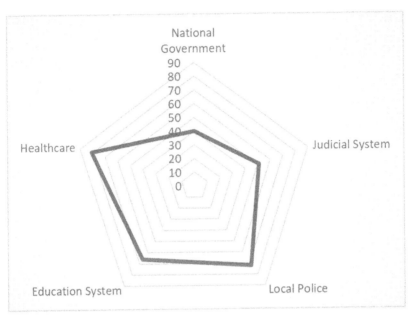

Figure 2: Trust in institutions
Source: After OECD (2013).

Why, if we are doing a better job of governing in some objective sense, is government seen as less trustworthy? Why do people not trust their national governments as much as they used to? As a psychologist, my major research interest is investigating this disconnect. My major research interest is to understand what exactly is happening with trust in government. Specifically, I study what is going on in citizens' experiences with government that might account for this erosion of trust.

A good place to start is to consider what the experience of government is like for most people. I will return to hard science later in this chapter, but I want to start framing the issue with two narratives about my own personal experiences with a private and a public organisation. The first experience—the private organisation experience—involved purchasing an iPad from an Apple Store. The other experience—the public organisation experience—involved taking my son to get a passport. His passport had expired and he was about to spend a university semester abroad studying in New Zealand. I think there are some interesting contrasts between these two experiences that illustrate some potential problem in how people experience their governments.

Let me start with the iPad experience. I decided I needed a new iPad, so I went to my local Apple Store: a bright, sunny building with lots of open space and large windows in the front. My first view of the store included all sorts of pictures and posters in the windows showing happy people enjoying the various electronic devices that could be purchased there. When you walk into an Apple Store—at least in Durham, North Carolina—you are immediately greeted by someone wearing an Apple T-shirt. The person who greets you is most likely a highly tattooed and much-pierced young person, but he or she is quite knowledgeable about Apple devices, as well as being highly trained in how to interact with you.

Apple Store employees are quite carefully taught skills such as how to greet potential customers. There is a well-designed and well-executed process that is used to pass a customer from the first salesperson encountered to the salesperson who specialises in the category of products that matches the customer's interest. When I entered the store, I was immediately approached and welcomed by a young man who introduced himself as 'Daniel'. Daniel welcomed me to the Apple Store and asked me how he could help me. When I told him I was interested in buying an iPad, Daniel told me 'Mark' was one of the store's iPad specialists. Daniel then explained that Mark was currently with another customer, but that if I would 'wait at this table'—where, incidentally, I could play with other Apple devices that I might also like to purchase—Mark would be with me shortly. Sure enough, in a few minutes Mark came over and talked to me about what I needed. He asked how I would be using my new iPad, explained the options available to me and advised me about what sort of services I might want. Mark made a point of mentioning, in an apparently a casual aside, that he was not paid on any commission, so I would know that he had no personal stake in my choice of product. He seemed to want me to find the iPad that was best for me. I walked out with an iPad and a memory of a positive experience with Apple. Now I am a business school professor—I know Apple does not really have an emotional need for me to like them. But they do—for business purposes—have a need to have a relationship with me, and they want me to feel good about my experience with their company. Judging by my personal experience, they execute that business strategy quite well.

Now let us consider my second example. My son Pippin and I went to our local post office to get his passport. The Chapel Hill post office building is not as striking as the Apple Store, but it is a pleasant enough location. The post office, like the Apple Store, had an attractive sign inviting and informing us about the product we were seeking, this sign told us that passports were available here at the post office and it directed us to the door of the passport office. Unfortunately, when we arrived at the passport office things got a bit less inviting. We were confronted with a closed and locked door displaying a sign that read: 'Passport applications must be completed before the appointment time and in black ink only'. The word 'before' was written in red and underlined twice. Beneath that sign was another that read: 'By appointment only'. And beneath that was a third sign that said: 'Knock twice'. The implication was clear: if you do not have an appointment, we do not want to see you. If you have not already completed your passport application, we do want to see you. And, by the way, knock twice because we are not going to be paying much attention to your needs, so you had better make them very well known if you expect us to respond.

Fortunately, Pippin had made an appointment online, and he had already downloaded and completed his passport application. Good citizen that he is, he had even used black ink. He knocked twice, and after what seemed a long time, the door was opened by a postal service employee who was of a similar age to the Apple employees who helped me buy the iPad. Unlike the Apple folks, though, she was not particularly friendly. She checked Pippin's forms and executed her part of the application-processing task competently, but she did so without a smile or any real personal engagement. The only remark she made that was even close to being individualised was an observation that Pippin's hair in the passport photo might be too long to be accepted by the State Department. The hair concern notwithstanding, in due time, Pippin got his new passport.

It occurred to me afterwards that these two experiences capture the essence of—and suggest a possible remedy for—some of the problems government has in building or maintaining public trust. For Pippin and me, the visit to the post office represented one of very few personal interactions we have with our national government. I pay my federal income taxes each year, but I do so without directly interacting with the government: my accountant prepares my tax forms and tells me how much to write the cheque for or, nowadays, gives the government permission to withdraw the amount due straight from my bank account.

My personal, *human* experience with the US Government is limited to interactions like the one Pippin and I had at the post office. (I should note that in the US many routine government interactions—applying for or renewing a driver's licence, for example, are interaction with state, county or city governments.)

Now why did the US Department of State treat us this way? Why did they not show any of the interest in building a relationship that was so obvious at the Apple Store? I think the reason is that while Apple knows they want us to come back and buy more Apple devices and therefore they see the value in inviting us to maintain a relationship with Apple, the Department of State does not see itself as competing for our business. If you are an American, where else are you going to get a passport? The passport office is without competition, or at least most policymakers would think that to be the case.

I want to argue, though, that the Department of State is wrong about this. What many of the people who make policy and design government procedures do not seem to understand (or have not thought through) is that citizens, the 'consumers' of government, in fact do have another option. They can choose to withdraw their trust in and engagement with the government; they can 'leave' psychologically even though they remain in the country by deciding to give the government less of their personal support. In organisational scholarship, we have the concept of 'organisational withdrawal', a common response of employees who feel they are receiving unfair or inconsiderate treatment by their employer. An employee who feels mistreated might not be able to leave their job because they do not have other employment opportunities, but they can withdraw psychologically. These workers simply withdraw, spending less and less time actually working and showing less and less diligence in what work they do. Workers who withdraw psychologically work only when they have to and only when they are sure that they will be paid for each and every effort. Similarly, a citizen who has withdrawn psychologically from their relationship with their government will only obey laws when enforcement is certain and they will not 'take on faith' the truth of what the government tells them about the state of the world. In short, they will not trust their government.

I have to admit that, after our experience at the passport office, I felt a tug of this sort of negative feeling about the US Government. For myself, I did not give in to that 'tug' of resentment partly because many years ago

I worked for the federal government and partly because I still have many friends who work in policymaking and policy research for governments around the world. From these experiences and acquaintances, I know that my government is staffed by hard-working, dedicated people. Therefore, I reminded myself that the way the local passport office was set up—as an adjunct to the post office staffed by workers who were trained in postal, not passport, duties—was probably the result of an attempt to save money on passport services. I considered in addition that the absence of any real customer service training, which was evident in the behaviour of the young woman at the passport office, was due to the pervasive government preoccupation with squelching fraud and waste, with the result that she was probably trained only to make sure the forms were correct. In short, it seemed likely that our passport office experience was the result of a government that gives cost savings and fraud prevention very high priority and relationship building very low priority. Note that Apple, which has to make money, not just save money, to continue to exist, has discovered that giving too much attention to cost savings and too little attention to relationship building is not, in fact, good for their bottom line.

Now let me shift from these stories of personal experiences to science. Viewed from the perspective of several decades of work in social and political psychology, my different reactions to the Apple Store and the passport office are not at all surprising. Beginning in the early 1970s, these sciences began to see evidence that people experiencing encounters with government are affected by more than just the material rewards and costs associated with the encounter, that they react at least as strongly to how they feel they have been treated. Work by a number of scholars has shown that whether one studies litigant reactions to legal procedures or citizen reactions to lawmaking and law enforcement, the belief that one has been treated in a fair, straightforward and inclusive way has profound effects on later attitudes and behaviour. In the 1970s and 1980s, research I conducted with colleagues at the US Federal Judicial Center, at the University of Illinois, and at the RAND Corporation showed that litigants in civil cases were more willing to accept legal decisions and more likely to trust federal courts if they felt they had received fair, inclusive and dignified treatment.

At about the same time, research conducted by Tom Tyler and his students and colleagues at Northwestern University and the University of California at Berkeley showed that citizens accepted and obeyed laws more if they believed that the law-making process was fair and provided them with opportunities for voice and inclusion. In the years since those early studies, additional research, including some quite good studies done recently in Australia, has shown that in contexts ranging from traffic stops to interactions with tax offices to civil and criminal trials, citizen reactions to government are affected profoundly by the process and treatment the citizen experiences. I will elaborate more on these lines of research below, but first I would like to describe some very recent studies that show just how deeply embedded are concerns with inclusive and fair treatment. I should note before I begin describing this work that a great deal of work, going back to the studies I just mentioned, has shown that there is a very close psychological connection between feelings of fair treatment and feelings of inclusion and, in the negative, between feelings of unfair treatment and feelings of exclusion.

Let me describe some findings from the new and growing field of neurological studies of social behaviour. This research studies in detail how the human brain works. First, consider that the human brain is in fact the organ through which all government works. We can make laws and policies, but ultimately everything depends on people understanding, evaluating and deciding whether to comply. That said, let's consider how the brain works in guiding behaviour. We human beings have a section at the front of our brain that is quite remarkable among animal species. This 'forebrain' is where we do maths and where we resolve problems of logic. This part of the brain is what makes economics work, by weighing individual benefits and costs and deciding which actions are in one's self-interest and which are not. But this is only part of the human brain, and it is only part of the story of how we make decisions and guide our behaviour. We humans also have another, important, portion of our brain, a part of the brain that evolved earlier but which is just as powerful. That part of the brain deals with social relationships.

The social part of the brain is preoccupied with how the person is being treated and what that treatment means for inclusion in important social groups and relationships. It plays a huge role in how we respond to people, groups and governments. There is some fascinating research on brain functioning that was published recently by Naomi Eisenberger, Matthew Lieberman and their colleagues and students at the University of California Los Angeles. In one set of studies, published in the journal *Science*. Eisenberger et al. (2003) recruited research participants and asked them to be the targets of functional magnetic resonance imaging (fMRI) while they were exposed to social experiences. fMRI machines are brain scanners that reveal what part of the brain is activated when the person being scanned is receiving a given stimulus experience. In this set of studies, the researchers exposed the participants to a computer game called Cyberball.

The game works like this: imagine you are lying in the fMRI machine, and you are asked to play a game of 'catch' on the computer screen in front of your face. The participants were told that there were two other participants (in other fMRI machines) who were playing the game with them. The game consists of catching the ball when it is thrown to you and then passing the ball to one of the other players. You operate a 'joystick' that controls a hand on a screen, and your movement of the joystick determines to whom you will throw the ball. (In fact, there was only the one participant—the behaviour of other two 'players' was in fact coded into the game software.) At first, the three players seemed to throw the ball to each other in a circular game of 'catch', with each player, including the real participant, catching the ball and then passing it on to the next person. After a while, though, the real participant found that the other two players began to pass the ball back and forth only to each other—the real participant was never again given the ball!

Eisenberger and her colleagues did this to see what the human brain does when the person is excluded—when he or she feels no longer 'part of the game'. What the researchers observed is that a specific part of the brain is activated when the participant is excluded—a brain area known as the anterior cingulate cortex. Once the participant was excluded from the game, more blood began flowing to that part of the brain. Now, what makes this finding remarkable and relevant to the topic under consideration here is that previous studies had shown that the anterior cingulate cortex is the part of the brain that is activated when participants are asked to stick their fingers into scalding water. This area is one of the brain's pain centres, a part of the brain that tells us we are hurt.

Eisenberger, Lieberman and their colleagues argue that this colocation of exclusion reactions and physical pain reactions makes sense because we have evolved as social animals and both exclusion and pain are important sensory cues. There was a time in our evolutionary history when being excluded from important groups meant one did not live very long. Consequently, early humans were more likely to survive if they developed a strong negative reaction to feeling excluded. As we evolved, the brain started using something it already had—the pain centre—to guide reactions to feelings of exclusion. Lieberman and Eisenberger point out that the comparisons that equate exclusion with pain are not just metaphors. Exclusion does not just *feel like* pain, the experience of exclusion *is* pain.

Other studies from this laboratory and other neuroscience labs show that just as feelings of inclusion activate a pain centre in the brain, the experience of fair treatment activates a pleasure centre. These neuroscience findings comport well with an older literature in social psychology, which had documented many instances where exclusion and unfair treatment makes people angry and combative while inclusion and fair treatment makes them cooperative and happier. Both lines of research suggest that if government can structure its interactions with citizens so that they feel included and fairly treated, it can provide direct and immediate benefits just by paying attention to how people are treated, simply by increasing inclusiveness and perceived fairness in the interaction.

With this immediate benefit of avoiding feelings of exclusion and promoting feelings of fair treatment in mind, we might ask a) how specifically government could promote such feelings, and b) what other positive consequences fair and inclusive procedures might have? A common argument in modern democracies is that citizens are de facto included in government decision-making and therefore treated fairly because they can vote on who makes and enforces the law. However, voting is a very indirect sort of inclusion, psychologically speaking. In the last US presidential election, for example, my vote represented approximately 1/136,000,000th of the decision-making control over the outcome—and that does not even consider the effects of the Electoral College system we have in the United States. In addition, knowing that one can vote is a forebrain, logical cognition: we understand, on a logical level, that if enough people like me vote in a particular way, we will change our government. Inclusion and fairness are more dependent on social brain than on forebrain processes; however, so *knowing* one can vote might not promote *feeling* that one is included in the body politic. The visit to the passport office I described earlier was a social brain kind of experience. The challenge in modern democracies is to find ways to build a greater feeling of inclusion and involvement with respect to national government. Voting is an important political right, but the research I just described, and that which I will describe below, suggests that we need to do more.

Neuroscience studies show a biological basis for strong negative reactions to exclusion and strong positive reactions to fairness. The social psychological research yields the same conclusions. It is worth delving deeper into exactly how feelings of inclusion and feelings of fair treatment are linked. The connection is seen in an area that is called the psychology of 'procedural justice'. Some years ago, Tom Tyler and I sought to explain why exactly people often respond more strongly to the processes they experience than to the outcomes they receive (Lind and Tyler 1988). Our explanation, included in what we termed 'Group Value Theory', was that being treated fairly by those in authority or those who are the representatives of an important institution or organisation gives people a sign that they are included in the social bonds and boundaries of the social institution in question.

For this reason, we argued, as fair treatment increases the feeling of inclusion increases. Tyler and I proposed that feelings of inclusion in turn prompt a variety of other psychological reactions—people who feel fairly treated (and who therefore feel included) are more cooperative, they more readily accept the authorities in the institution and obey the decisions those authorities make, they are more likely to comply with the rules of the institution, and they have greater trust in the authorities and in the institution. On the other hand, people who feel unfairly treated (and therefore feel excluded) will be less cooperative, they will accept authorities and decisions less, they will be less likely to comply with rules, and they will trust the institution less. In the 30 years since Tom and I published our theory (and an extension of the theory called the 'Relational Model of Authority') (Lind and Tyler 1988), there have been many studies testing both the basic proposition that perceived fairness prompts feelings of inclusion and the additional propositions that, because of this connection with inclusion, feelings of fair treatment lead to greater compliance, obedience and trust. The results—some of which I will describe below—have been right in line with what we theorised.

Figure 3 presents some recent data some colleagues and I collected on this often-observed pattern of connections between perceived fairness, inclusion and trust. In this study, we asked people whether they felt they had been treated fairly, whether they felt included in the system and its processes and decisions, and whether they trusted the authority with whom they had worked. As can be seen from the graphs, as perceptions of fair process increased so did feelings of inclusion, and as feelings of inclusion increased so did trust.

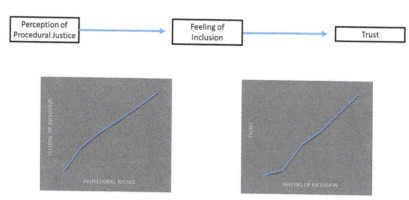

Figure 3: Perceptions of justice, inclusion and trust
Source: Lind and Sitkin (2018).

If fair treatment fosters a feeling of inclusion and this builds trust in government, how might we increase feelings of fairness in citizen–government interactions? Since much of the research documenting the link between fairness and trust has focused on procedural justice judgements, we would probably do best to look at how we might build feelings of procedural fairness. Let me note at the outset that procedural fairness judgements are not judgements about abstract fairness. They are judgements about how fairly one views some personal experience with government. These procedural fairness judgements tend to be influenced mainly by the rules and nuances of treatment encountered in an interaction with government, not so much by whether the ultimate outcome of the encounter was favourable or unfavourable. Procedural fairness judgements are also different to satisfaction. Immediate satisfaction with an interaction with government often has a stronger outcome component, but satisfaction reactions are also transient, and less enduring, than are procedural fairness judgements. Research in a variety of government contexts shows that satisfaction does not influence trust in government as much as procedural justice judgements do.

Four decades of research on procedural justice has identified some procedural and process elements that reliably increase the feeling that one has been treated fairly. This body of research shows four major features of an interaction with government that drive perceptions of fair treatment and, through fairness judgements, the feeling of inclusion. Three of these factors are especially relevant to interaction with government agencies in societies that are not prone to government corruption. In societies or nations where government processes, officials and decisions are open to corruption or bias, of course, the absence of such bias is also central, indeed often key, to whether the process is seen as fair. In most citizen–government interactions in nations with fair degrees of transparency and without much corruption, the 'big three' fairness features are 'voice', respect and dignity, and explanations. 'Voice' refers to whether the individual is allowed to express his or her views, evidence and perspective, and whether the government authority shows evidence of considering these things. Respect and dignity as features of process refer to whether the authority treats the individual as a full person, with the respect for his or her decisions and with the dignity that everyone has a right to expect. The third feature—explanations—has to do with whether the authority or the government has explained in a comprehensible fashion how the process will unfold, how decisions will be made and why things are structured the way they are.

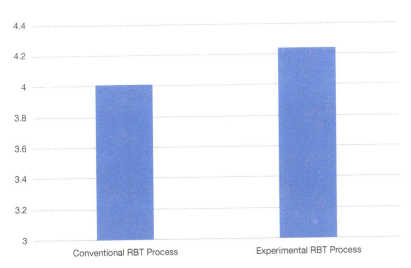

Figure 4: Perceived procedural fairness ratings

Note: RBT = Random Breath Testing

Source: After Mazerolle, Bennett, Antrobus and Eggins (2012).

Some recent research on alcohol breath-testing stops by police in Queensland, Australia, provides an excellent example of how government–citizen interactions can be modified to enhance citizen's perceptions of fair treatment. This research was conducted by Professor Lorraine Mazerolle of the University of Queensland and her colleagues, Sarah Bennett, Emma Antrobus and Elizabeth Eggins. In this Queensland Community Engagement Trial (QCET), the researchers, collaborating with the local police, created an experimental script to guide police actions when they made a random drink-driving stop. The police and the researchers were careful to include all of the 'big three' fairness elements in the experimental script for the traffic stop, and they compared drivers' reactions to this experimental script to reactions to the conventional process and actions used in these sorts of stops.

In the QCET experimental process—the fair process condition—when the police officer approached the driver's car, he or she explained to the motorist why they had been stopped. It was not the motorist's driving that prompted the stop, the officer explained, but rather simply because they had been randomly selected for breath testing. Thus, the process began with a clear explanation of the reason for the stop. The officer continued by explaining what would happen during and after the breath testing. While the officer was giving this explanation and throughout the interaction at the motorist's car, the experimental process dictated that the officer should squat down so that he or she would be looking eye-to-eye with the seated motorist rather than looking down from a standing posture. These behavioural nuances and special attention to the use of polite language and demeanour by the officer were designed to convey a message of respect. Finally, as the stop progressed, the office asked the motorist to voice his or her opinion and views. Specifically, the officer asked what the driver being stopped thought should be done about drink driving.

Because the QCET study used a randomised research design, the researchers could make a strong and direct comparison between the fairness judgements engendered by the experimental process and the conventional process. Figure 4 shows the results—the experimental process produced more positive fairness experiences than did the conventional process. Here, in a real-world everyday government–citizen context, it was possible to make people feel more fairly treated just by modifying the process to incorporate voice, respect and explanations. It is not difficult to imagine how governments could make similar changes in process to enhance the experience of citizens across a wide variety of interactions with government agencies and offices.

Now let us consider what benefits might be realised if governments were to make these changes. Here, too, the research literature provides evidence of what might happen if the process and procedures of citizen–government interactions are such that they enhance feelings of fair treatment. First, improving perceived fairness would build trust in government and increase perceptions of the legitimacy of the government. I began this chapter with some data that show decreased trust in government across the OECD member nations in general, and in Australia and the US in particular. If we enhanced trust and legitimacy by increasing feelings of fair treatment on citizen interaction at the time, we might be able to reverse these disturbing trends

A study reported by Tom Tyler, Lawrence Sherman, Heather Strang, Geoffrey Barnes and Daniel Woods (2007) provides a nice example of how attention to fairness in the design of government procedures can enhance legitimacy and trust. This study, which was part of a restorative justice program in Canberra, examined the effects of a new procedure for dealing with habitual drink-driving cases, comparing the new procedure to the existing procedures used in such cases. The new process was designed to include the procedural justice elements of voice, respect and dignity, and explanations as well as other features that could help the offender become reintegrated into his or her family and community.

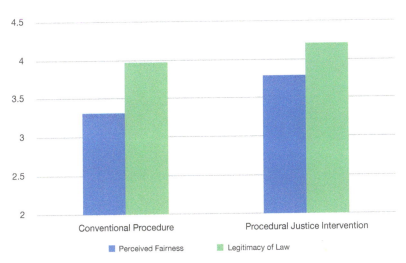

Figure 5: Perceived fairness and legitimacy in the Canberra RISE experiment
Source: After Tyler, Sherman, Strang, Barnes and Woods (2007).

Figure 5 shows the results of the RISE experiment. When the enhanced procedural fairness process was used, there was an increase in perceived fairness on the part of both the defendant and the defendant's families, and there was a corresponding increase in endorsements of the legitimacy of existing drunk-driving laws. This experiment demonstrates that it is possible to make people more trusting of government and more accepting of its legitimacy just by adding perceived fairness considerations into the design of process and procedures. Additional research by Tyler and other scholars have shown this strong connection between trust and legitimacy and perceptions of fair treatment in citizen–government interactions.

A second reason that governments would be well advised to design processes and procedures to enhance perceptions of fair treatment has to do with improving citizens' compliance with and acceptance of laws, rules and decisions. Early in my career, when I worked for the US Federal Judiciary and later for the RAND Corporation, I did a great deal of research on the question of what induces litigants to accept a judicial judgement rather than appeal the decision or simply not comply with it. Those studies, as well as research by other scholars, showed that acceptance of judicial and quasi-judicial decisions is strongly linked to the perception of fair process. Remarkably, the impact of procedural fairness judgements on acceptance of decisions is strong whether people win or lose their case. Even litigants who lose tend to accept and comply with the judge's or hearing officer's decision as long as they feel they were treated fairly in the legal process.

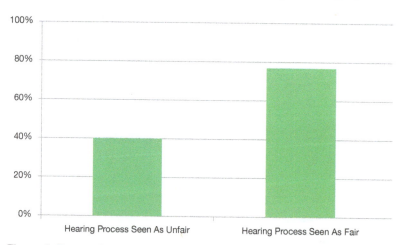

Figure 6: Perceptions of fairness in court-annexed arbitration procedures
Source: After Lind, Kulik, Ambrose and Park (1993).

An example of this fairness effect can be seen in the research findings shown in Figure 6, which shows the results of studies on court-annexed arbitration procedures in the US federal courts. Carol Kulik, Maureen Ambrose, Maria de Vera Park and I studied what drove decisions to accept arbitrators' judgements in tort and contract cases subject to mandatory arbitration in federal district (trial) courts. We were interested in whether litigants' judgements of the fairness of the hearing process affected whether they would accept the arbitrators' judgements. (Under this version of arbitration, either party to a dispute could, at their discretion, reject the arbitration award and opt for a full trial.) The cases in question involved substantial amounts in controversy—up to several hundred thousand dollars. The findings were quite remarkable: even in these large disputes, feelings of fair treatment exerted strong influence on whether the arbitrator's judgement was accepted or appealed.

The link between perceptions of fair process and compliance was also seen in a recent study of pre-promulgation hearing procedures used to gather input for the design of government regulations. The regulation process studied in this research involved the creation of new rules governing pollutants in a major river system in my home state of North Carolina. The regulations under consideration would restrict how cities on the river could dispose of effluents and how farmers with fields along the river could fertilise crops. A series of public hearings were held to gather stakeholder and citizen input. My former student Kelly See studied how perceptions of the hearing process affected willingness to accept the regulations that the state government ultimately enacted. Figure 7 shows some of See's findings: hearing attendees who viewed the process as fair were more willing to accept the new regulations than were those who did not think the process was fair.

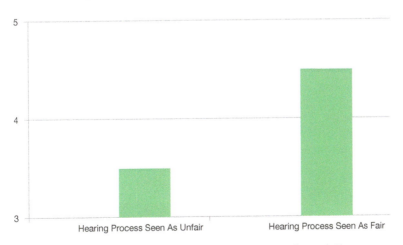

Figure 7: Perceptions of fairness and acceptance of regulations
Source: After See (2009).

I started this chapter with the assertion that many modern governments are *doing* the job of governing well, but they are not *seen* as doing their job well—at least they are not seen as trustworthy. I have reviewed the science on the social brain and the science on the psychology of perceived fairness because I think that at least part of the solution to the problem of growing distrust might be to pay more attention to improving citizens' personal experience with government. (I have only mentioned a few of the many relevant studies here, but interested readers can find more detailed descriptions and a useful bibliography in an OECD expert paper I authored with Christiane Arndt (Lind and Arndt 2016).) Research like that I have described here makes it clear that governments could increase citizen trust one interaction at a time, if they changed the procedures and processes used in citizen-facing policies and if they trained their staff to attend not only to administering laws and policies correctly but also to doing so in a respectful, clear and engaging manner.

References

Eisenberger, N.I., M.D. Lieberman and K.D. Williams. 2003. 'Does Rejection Hurt? An fMRI Study of Social Exclusion'. *Science* 302(5643): 290–92. doi.org/10.1126/science.1089134

Lind, E. and C. Arndt. 2016. 'Perceived Fairness and Regulatory Policy: A Behavioural Science Perspective on Government-Citizen Interactions'. *OECD Regulatory Policy Working Papers*, No. 6. Paris: OECD Publishing. doi.org/10.1787/1629d397-en

Lind, E., C.T. Kulik, M. Ambrose and M.V. de Vera. Park. 1993. 'Individual and Corporate Dispute Resolution: Using Procedural Fairness as a Decision Heuristic'. *Administrative Science Quarterly* 38(2): 224–51. doi.org/10.2307/2393412

Lind, E. and S. Sitkin. 2018. *The Six Domains of Leadership*. Columbia, SC: Learning with Leaders, p. 57.

Lind, E. and T.R. Tyler. 1988. *The Social Psychology of Procedural Justice*. New York: Plenum Press.

Mazerolle, L., S. Bennett, E. Antrobus and E. Eggins. 2012. 'Procedural Justice, Routine Encounters and Citizen Perceptions of Police: Main Findings from the Queensland Community Engagement Trial (QCET)'. *Journal of Experimental Criminology* 8(4): 343–67. doi.org/10.1007/s11292-012-9160-1

Organisation for Economic Co-operation and Development (OECD). 2013. 'Government at a Glance 2013'. OECD: Paris. Available from www.oecd-ilibrary.org/governance/government-at-a-glance-2013/confidence-in-national-government-in-2012-and-its-change-since-2007_gov_glance-2013-graph1-en

See, K.E. 2009. 'Reactions to Decisions with Uncertain Consequences: Reliance on Perceived Fairness Versus Predicted Outcomes Depends on Knowledge'. *Journal of Personality and Social Psychology* 96(1): 104–18. doi.org/10.1037/a0013266

Tyler, T., L. Sherman, H. Strang, G. Barnes and D. Woods. 2007. 'Reintegrative Shaming, Procedural Justice, and Recidivism: The Engagement of Offenders' Psychological Mechanisms in the Canberra RISE Drinking-and-Driving Experiment'. *Law & Society Review* 41(3): 553–86. doi.org.10.1111/j.1540-5893.2007.00314.x

9

More than just a five-minute conversation: A case study in civic engagement from Germany

Dominik Hierlemann

It is Winston Churchill who is widely misattributed as saying that 'the best argument against democracy is a five-minute conversation with the average voter'. And yet, in a time when populist movements are gaining increasing support, undoubtedly some readers will find an element of truth to this misquote. As a matter of fact, politicians desperately need to have more than just a five-minute conversation with the average voter in order to strengthen and rejuvenate democracy. In fact, I will present a project from 2011 when two German foundations conducted a thorough conversation with more than 10,000 average voters: the so-called Citizens' Forum (Bertelsmann Stiftung and Heinz Nixdorf Stiftung. 2014).

To put this public participation project into perspective, I would like to begin with a brief reflection on how Germany is perceived from the outside. Probably 'not too bad' might be the short answer to such a question. Germany's economy under Chancellor Angela Merkel is thriving. Looking simply at statistics, the general level of trust in government is relatively high compared to other countries. But from the inside perspective, the picture is quite different. In fact, there is not much of a difference between Germany and most Western countries.

Recognising disjuncture

Germany, like many other Western nations, is experiencing a growing gap between politicians and the electorate. People are dissatisfied with how political decisions are made and, although they are still interested in politics—this, to me, is the interesting point—they are no longer interested in political parties or the way politics works. Taking a more theoretical approach, it is possible to say that the politics of delivery is coming to an end. Until recently, the working mode has been as follows: citizens were there to provide votes, politicians delivered results and citizens were perceived as clients; now this circular logic has fundamentally changed.

One of the major catalysts of the emergence of new forms of public participation in Germany—or of deliberative democracy approaches as it is also referred to in the academic community—was widespread discontentment about the non-involvement in big infrastructure projects. The case of Stuttgart 21, where literally hundreds of thousands of people rallied against plans to build a new underground train station is exemplary. It was not simply a case of 'not in my backyard' (NIMBY) citizens that took to the streets, but something much bigger. Citizens were obviously dissatisfied with how the planning process of an infrastructure project was being conducted. Moreover, and more significantly, they felt a systemic exclusion of political processes with far-reaching results.

It was around this time the Bertelsmann Stiftung (Foundation) decided to develop a new approach to engage citizens in politics. There were already many methods out there, of course, and many were already being applied in Australia and New Zealand. So the foundation, with its partners, did not aim at developing a totally new and different approach but rather aimed to make sure that whatever method was chosen fit the current situation in Germany. But we were not revolutionaries: the ultimate goal was and still is to complement our representative democracy, not to develop a substitute.

The overall rationale for the project was: how can we reduce the gap between politics and citizens? This may not sound very ambitious, but I still believe it is the single most important issue when we talk about citizen engagement. How can we, if not eliminate the gap, then at least reduce it? How can we have more channels of communication between citizens and politicians? A critical point to make here is that many participation projects that are initiated by governmental bodies on all levels have the sole aim of generating acceptance for decisions that have already been made. Clearly, this leads to even more frustration.

In communicating with their citizens, politicians should ideally start from the point of saying 'yes'. However, most often their focus is different. They are often more concerned about communication styles, communication forms and all sorts of new social media instruments that help them to deliver their message more clearly. Their impetus is rather 'yes, how can we convince citizens?' They wish to communicate their message better, not engage with citizens in a different way.

The Forum dynamics

The Citizens' Forum took place in 2011. It was a nationwide public participation project, and one of our central aims was to strengthen the democratic skills of citizens, to awaken or to revitalise political interest.

Democracy, we thought, needed new venues. When I had a discussion a while ago with a German minister, he complained that while he was travelling throughout his constituency, he always seemed to be meeting the same people. We may well think that this minister was not going to the right places; however, it was equally true that it was always the same types of people who were engaged in the traditional forms of politics.

One way we combated this was by holding the Citizens' Forum in 25 different places and—even more importantly—participants were selected at random. So we had 10,000 participants; 400 in each region. They were invited by the Federal President who initiated the project at the time— which, though attractive at the time, led to some problems I will explore shortly.

And although it has been, until this point, the biggest project of its kind in Germany, some perspective must be kept. I recently met a woman from a Chinese non-government organisation who is doing a public participation project in China. When I told her we had 10,000 participants, she said that would be a bus stop in China.

The Citizens' Forum consisted of three key features. First of all, participants were randomly selected. This is critically important, but it also consumes a lot of time—not to mention money. We considered it important that, through this approach, as many heterogeneous perspectives as possible flowed into the forum so as to avoid the scenario of the minister in Germany I mentioned who just met the usual suspects. In order to achieve that, we worked with a call centre: they randomly selected participants, telephoned them and said, 'we're calling you on behalf of the Federal President'. People were informed on the phone about the project and they had an opportunity to look up a website with more details.

Still, many people hung up straight away. Others were happy to stay on the line for a good chat but then said, 'well, you're talking about politics, I'll get you my husband'. But we wanted to make sure that we had different perspectives, so we had three criteria: gender, educational status and age—because while it was easy to find a middle-aged engineer, it was quite difficult to get in touch with a young woman from East Germany with a low level of education. We had to conduct many phone calls in order to get such demographics in our forum.

The next feature was that we had a combination of offline and online activities. We started with a one-day opening event, followed by an online discussion, and finally a closing event at the end of an eight-week period. This timeframe and structure was important, as it meant people got to know each other quite well at the forum. The discussion culture at the Citizens' Forum distinguished itself significantly from discussions on newspaper online forums or anything else you will find on the web. Participants showed respect to one another and behaved in a way that allowed others to easily and willingly join discussions.

People also became familiar with the process during the day and it suited different participation needs or individuals' strengths. For example, men tended to do well in our 'world cafés', a method where people changed tables in order to get to know different perspectives, but senior citizens and female participants became quite engaged in our online discussion. Although participants were online, they did not only discuss online— they worked online to try to put a common text together. And this was the focus of the forum: the way our website was organised ensured that, by the end of the project, participants would have produced a written program.

In other words, the Citizens' Forum was not just for the sake of discussion. There was a tangible result, a program at the end of the day. At the time in 2011, the topic of our forum was how we could foster social cohesion in our society. Participants had a choice of six different committees ranging from educational policy over immigration issues to future forms of democratic engagement. The main work of the forum took place in these committees. This way they were not engaging with 10,000 other citizens or even 400 other citizens. Instead, participants engaged within a group of 50 or 60 different citizens, because we believed this was the group size where you could still get to know each other well and where it would still be possible to work on a common text.

It was important to create a sense of community right from the start. And, as in real life, we needed a kind of dramatic structure of events: participants needed a warming-up phase so they had the opportunity to get to know the website and how the online forum worked before they engaged in a discussion in our online forum. Moreover, the events were organised in a kind of world café format so that participants could hear from different people and get to know different perspectives.

In our world café setting, a group of up to six people sat at a table, engaging in a discussion. We had so-called table hosts, people who stayed at the table and told new arrivals to the table what had happened so far. People moved around the room and, at the end of the day, they came up with different thoughts and ideas. The committees were separated by pinboards, where voting for ideas took place. In this way, the discussion was funnel-shaped: many ideas at the beginning and then, at the end of the day, just four bullet points, which were suggestions based on the ideas.

This was the starting point for the online discussion. Because it was our belief that you cannot start an online discussion with a blank page. And so our participants were given their event results as starting points for their discussion and work that they were doing online.

Let us now come to the online deliberation. What did the website look like? First of all, we believed it was important there be a personal component involved. For this reason, participants entered the discussion with their real name and a portrait; this way, they knew, amongst themselves, whether they had met or not. Through the use of a kind of social media component, we could make the experience more convenient and familiar to participants. Moreover, the online deliberation was facilitated by former participants of our pilot projects.

We didn't pay facilitators. Ordinary citizens facilitated the whole online deliberation. It was also important that we did not interfere in terms of content. It was left up to the participants to determine the content. In doing so, I think we were quite unique, because often there is a certain degree of guidance there.

Nevertheless, I would say our approach was structured very well. Because we wanted to make sure that after six to eight weeks, ultimately, results were being delivered. While we did not interfere in terms of content, we made sure all participants walked away with their result. To help achieve this, participants had to complete certain tasks. Initially some of them did not like this; the older participants tended to say 'homework—that's twenty years ago'.

But we were adamant that certain tasks be completed. Some took just five minutes. We explained the importance of this to be retention: normally, when starting an online discussion, people became involved very quickly, they participated actively for a couple of days. After that, participation usually declined equally fast. So how could we make sure that the level of participation remained high throughout the entire project? The solution was to intervene at least structurally from time to time. Organisers needed to get in touch with participants from time to time. For example, in the middle of our forum we phoned participants and asked them how they were finding it, whether they wanted to participate a little more actively and so on.

In our experience, the elderly were often especially fascinated with the internet. This cuts to the issue of the digital divide. Because while participants in our project who did not have a computer could go to the library, if they were not digital natives we needed to ensure that they received adequate training. From the experience of the Citizens' Forum, this did not tend to be a problem: while the younger, more internet-savvy generation can be critical of the online forum setup, elder citizens are increasingly becoming quite engaged and accepting.

The outcomes of our project were ideas and proposals on a range of topics connected to the question of how more social cohesion in German society could be achieved. Participants urged for a common nationwide educational policy, delivered concrete proposals on how to facilitate the integration of refugees on the local level, and developed far-reaching ideas like a state-guaranteed basic income. All of these topics were debated in a closing event with the Federal President in the former German Bundestag and in subsequent meetings with high-ranking politicians in Berlin. But they were also discussed on the regional level. In every one of these 25 forums, we had closing events, and the results of our project were discussed with councillors, mayors and members of parliament. And it was up to them, of course, whether they wanted to institute the results of the project in policy.

So what were the results of the project? At the beginning, expectations were high: when the Federal President is involved, people raise their expectations. Never mind that the President of Germany is a figurehead with few powers: the average person thinks that because they received an invitation from the Federal President, results from the forum will be implemented.

This means we often had to temper expectations. We made sure that citizens were familiar with the relevant political processes and we ensured some sort of procedural justice. What we told participants right from the beginning was that while we could not guarantee that any results of the projects would be implemented, we would make sure that participants had the chance and the opportunity to discuss results with relevant politicians.

The findings

Let me briefly share some insights I gained during this project. First of all, was online becoming the new normal? We conducted this project in 2011, when politicians were emphasising getting their message across online; nowadays, the emphasis is more specifically on social media. And yet, while this may be so, I would say the Citizens' Forum demonstrated the continued, strong desire for face-to-face engagement.

Consequently, we needed to create a mixture of face-to-face engagement and online deliberation. This could be done through different participation opportunities. We also needed to ensure we did not simply reach out to the usual suspects. Sometimes their participation is appropriate: if a new infrastructure project is to be built, for example, all relevant stakeholders need to be invited. Our impetus at the time was to get people from all walks of life, and to do so we needed to look beyond merely the well-educated, eloquent middle class who usually engage with the policymaking process.

This is not to say that such a process is all about peace, love and harmony, much as the stereotype of citizen engagement might imply this. Inevitably, some people will be disappointed with the results. Conflicts arise within groups. These must be dealt with. Most importantly, it is not possible to maintain control over the process as a whole—the precise reason why traditional policymakers are not very keen on the idea. But, on the other hand, this is the very thing that makes such a process so attractive.

Finally, I wish to end with one last insight: that there are of course different definitions of public or civic participation derived from different perspectives. For politicians, it is seen as a tool for more effective communication to improve their messaging. They merely want to get in touch with citizens in different ways but often try to involve them in direct decision-making processes. But when you speak with citizens, it becomes very clear that they want to be directly *involved* in decision-making. All organisers of public participation projects need to keep these different attitudes in mind. Organisers do not only need to bridge the gap between politicians and citizens; they first of all need to bridge the gap between the different expectations and the possible outcome of public participation projects.

References

Bertelsmann Stiftung and Heinz Nixdorf Stiftung. 2014. 'Citizens' Forum: Community Input and Discussion for Greater Impact'. Available from buerger-forum.info/download/BuergerForumA5_engl_2014_final.pdf

10

We hear you! Case studies in authentic civic engagement from the City of Melbourne

Stephen Mayne

This contribution to the present volume follows on from Dominik Hierlemann's earlier reflections on Germany's Citizens' Forum (Chapter 10). The City of Melbourne recently held a similar civic engagement experiment in public policymaking in the form of a citizen jury to help formulate our first-ever 10-year financial plan.

First, some background. At the City of Melbourne, we claim to be the most open and transparent local council in Australia. Some of the things we have done to justify this boast include fully disclosing our lease register and our individual land valuations. We also disclosed the contracts of our top six executives: their start date, their end date, what they are paid and so on. Moreover, we have a conflict of interest register on our website. Every time a councillor declares a conflict of interest for a political donation, it appears on the register. And we disclose, quarterly, all our expenses. Examples include public pre-approval of all interstate and international travel.

We also try and maintain a transparent decision-making process, with most of our tenders done in open session. To this end, we also allow public questions at the beginning and the end of every committee meeting: twice a month we have unscripted oral public questions, with no warning or notice. Audio of all council meetings and committee meetings is put online. As are all submissions from the community, so we can see what everyone else is saying. And we allow the community to participate in every single resolution at committee. They can submit 10 times in the one night on all different planning applications, if they wish, and then their submission is on the website as audio and a written submission on the website for everyone to see.

We still have a few things to achieve with regards to transparency. We are yet to work up a 10-year capital works program with detail so residents can see the individual projects: what are we spending in 2021–22, for instance. We need to be more open and transparent with our enterprise agreement. I would love to do a citizen jury on that. There has never been one done in Australia on enterprise agreements. And I would love to get councillors to admit how many free tickets we get to events. My colleagues have been very agreeable so far on transparency, but they don't all share my views on this specific issue. I may have to do that one just before the next election and embarrass them into admitting that we should disclose all free tickets that we receive to events. Because there is a lot of them.

Formulating a 10-year plan

The authorising environment for our first citizen jury was a community engagement framework. We have a council plan with eight goals listed in it, a declaration of the council values and then our vision statement to be 'bold, inspirational and sustainable'. It was at the start of the last council that we put in that aim to be Australia's most open and transparent council. In terms of our 10-year financial plan, we previously didn't have one. And one of the things about citizens' juries, as mentioned by Dominik Hierlemann in this volume, is that we have to give them real power. We cannot simply make a decision and then ask for retrospective approval. We have to put a decision on the line and let the community decide.

And so, having never formulated a 10-year financial plan, we decided to let the community have the first go. And because we had no previous such financial plan, there was no defence of the status quo among our councillors. There was no policy at all. In fact, previously in this area there had been very little transparency. We just had an annual budget. We did have a four-year forward estimate, but it was not very detailed.

So, the 10-year plan represented a new piece of disclosure and forward planning. We could have pursued the New York model of 'let's let them decide $2 million worth of grants in a ward'; that approach is easy: put a small bit of money on the table and let the community talk about a few visible projects like a new park and that sort of thing. But we thought we would get the community to start with their plan. That is a far more complex procedure.

To give readers an idea of numbers involved, our annual budget is around $430 million a year. We hold $4.5 billion in assets, and employ 1,200 staff. We have to spend $700 million on open space in the next 10 years. We are going to spend $250 million on the Queen Victoria Market—at 18 acres, the world's biggest open-air market. How are we going to fund it and not jack the rates up too much? We wanted to hear what the citizens' forum thought. One of the problems is that we are currently over-dependent on car parking revenue, from which we make $100 million per year. But, given the rapid changes to transportation, be it carpooling or driverless cars, this may fall in the future, meaning we need to diversify our revenue sources.

Consider some of the drivers of our 10-year financial plan. In the 2014–15 financial year, the City of Melbourne had the fastest growing population out of Australia's 560 councils. On the ground, this means massive density, massive apartment approvals and strong immigration. Melbourne, along with London, New York and Paris, is one of the world's four biggest cities for international students. The challenge of this amazing growth for us, the capital city council, is how we are going to manage and finance it.

By way of comparison, Sydney's Barangaroo redevelopment covers around 20 hectares. We have a couple of hundred hectares of urban renewal space when you combine Fishermans Bend, Arden-Macaulay and the rest of Docklands. These areas represent a lot of infill: former industrial areas with high density and strong growth. It is our job to manage the finances around it.

The Economist (2017) has declared Melbourne the world's most lovable city for the last seven years. How do we retain that title? We first asked our citizen jury. Next, more specifically, council officers put on the table that we were $900 million short in terms of our long-term projections of delivering infrastructure. At the time that was a controversial number from the administration because the Lord Mayor himself didn't believe it was true.

But this controversy was also a strength: the officers had to come up with a position. Previously, no one had said what the infrastructure shortfall was—because no one had ever asked or calculated it. We said to the officers we were getting 43 ordinary citizens to formulate a 10-year financial plan, and we wanted the officers to tell them what they thought the shortfall was. The officers had to dig their way through their spreadsheets and come up with a number that the Lord Mayor disputed. The fact that we had a jury deciding our policies for the next 10 years shows how successful the process is in eliciting much new information. It was a comprehensive engagement process. We had pop-ups, we had surveys, we had budget simulators. We conducted significant, preliminary engagement before we empanelled our 43 panellists.

The engagement process

How did we select them? We said we would have 50 per cent from our business electoral franchise and 50 per cent from our residential electoral franchise. In hindsight, the category that we omitted was the 700,000 people who visit the city every day: the workers, the international visitors—we did not give them a say. Perhaps that was why many of the recommendations that emerged were very anti-car, because we did not have anyone on the panel who was driving in or stuck in traffic, day after day.

We went for our voting franchises, which is people, residential and business, who could vote. We ensured that we had good diversity so we engaged with the universities to make sure we got lots of students involved, because 42 per cent of the residents in the City of Melbourne are students. We also went for diversity in geography, business, residential status, age and gender.

I have already mentioned the online budget simulator but not yet the funnel approach, whereby we presented the panel with a wad of research and feedback from what the community was already saying about our financial challenges before they even sat down. Using our online simulator, anyone can move a dial to indicate whether they support spending more on events and less on community services. That gave us some more interesting feedback, which we gave to the panel.

The panel was then assisted by the New Democracy Foundation, which is funded by Luca Belgiorno-Nettis, whose father was one of the founders of Transfield. He has donated about $5 million to the foundation because he believes the political system is broken, and that citizen juries are the way to make public policy. From our experience, I agree with him. There is a massive trust deficit for local government; the community thinks we are all hopeless and conflicted and corrupt. Because of this, it is wonderful to randomly select a jury, instead of engaging the usual suspects of squeaky wheels banging on, privileged rent seekers and those who know which buttons to push.

Moreover, our randomly selected jurors were committed. Over six full Saturdays—sunny Saturdays, too—they showed up. By the end, we thought we would be down to 30 participants, but we still had 43. They loved the fact that there was real policy on the line. They loved the fact that they could choose the topics and speakers, who they nominated by name. When they asked us about demography, for example, they requested News Corp social commentator Bernard Salt to speak to them and he did. When they told us they wanted to hear more about climate change from Monash University Professor Graeme Pearman, we invited him too.

It was up to participants to decide in which direction the process went. After the initial presentations from City of Melbourne officers, the panel then chose what they wanted to hear. They told us they wanted to hear from the planning minister. They picked the topics and we councillors had little influence—we were not allowed to intervene unless requested. The sessions were open to observers more than 90 per cent of the time, but only New Democracy and the facilitators from Mosaic Lab were allowed to attend all the sessions. Residents' groups were initially furious, but slowly came around as they came to watch a few sessions and were allowed to observe most of it, without ever campaigning or participating. There was a feedback board for written comments and suggestions, but we explained to them that no outside influences were permitted—as with a legal jury. For the same reason, the media were allowed to some sessions, but not the deliberative ones.

Council is a very complex beast, with five key service streams, meaning we had to explain to the citizen jury all the things we do. It was thus a huge task to get the community—with no initial knowledge—to understand the full complexity and diversity of a capital city council. And, in hindsight, it was probably almost too big a challenge in terms of getting people up to speed with all the details of what councils do. We also had to deliver them rates modelling and how we measure infrastructure spendings.

Outcomes

So what were the practical outcomes of this process? We all learnt so much from this amazing sharing and first-time disclosure of all this new information. The panel of citizen jurors made 11 recommendations. Melbourne City Council held a special committee meeting to receive the panel report and then we agreed to consider it more thoroughly; we adopted our first-ever 10-year plan on 30 June 2015. Moreover, we embedded the full panel report in our 10-year financial plan. And we made our officers explain their decisions behind implementing—or not— particular recommendations.

The panel was delighted because there was a very strong adherence in the 10-year plan to their recommendations. For example, I wanted to sell Citywide, the services company that we own—quite a big business, with $200 million in revenue. They panel said no. I thanked them, deferred to their decision and said we would not privatise Citywide. Instead, we are taking up their suggestion to review our property portfolio, as well as cranking up our developer contributions.

The City of Sydney has been making almost $100 million a year from developers in recent times. We have probably made $50 million in 20 years. We are severely under-taxing the developers. Consequently, we have now effectively doubled the revenue we are getting from open space contributions from developers. Normally, such a move would have been resisted by the Liberals and a few others, but because it was the citizen jurors who argued for this decision, it was passed unanimously a few weeks after the panel made their recommendations. They have delivered real influential outcomes.

Two more examples of this: we are cranking up our spending on renewables and sustainability because the panel said we should do it and we are going after car parking because they said we are too reliant on it, and we needed to get more cars out of the city. Two weeks after they said that, we established 20 car-free bays for motorcycles. We simply converted them from car to motorcycle use and sustained the resulting revenue loss. I was able to get that initiative passed by pointing out that it was a panel recommendation.

The citizen jury received positive media coverage, especially from ABC Radio National (Ryan 2015) and *The Age* (Reece 2015). Yes, some of the tabloid media, the *Herald Sun* among them (Reece 2014), attacked it at first. This is in part because they are privileged influences too: they like to be able to ring the Lord Mayor; they like to be able to write editorials that tell politicians how to behave.

But they changed their view when they realised we were involving real people—people who read the *Herald Sun*—who would tell us what to do. That argument tended to neutralise the critique that councillors are outsourcing their job because they cannot do it themselves—a popular accusation levelled at Julia Gillard when she announced her desire to hold a citizens' jury on climate change just before the 2010 election. She was heavily criticised for the perception she was copping out on a policy position where Labor was fully invested by trying to outsource it to a panel.

Finally, we did some research with the panellists under the auspices of the University of Melbourne. The panellists are now our biggest advocates. They go around telling people how great the City of Melbourne is. They say that they are very satisfied with democracy at the city council. One-third of them say they are much more interested in politics than they were previously. New Democracy has told us that, on average, one-third of participants in citizen juries end up then volunteering for something else because they have become engaged through the process. In other words, they have become civically stimulated.

People love to volunteer not only because they receive a gold embossed invitation from the Lord Mayor that looks like a royal wedding invitation, but because they love the fact that it is a finite commitment. You are not secretary of your local tennis club for life—you are volunteering for five or six Saturdays and then you can get on with your life. There is no ongoing commitment. So we were surprised that 700 of the 7,000 people we randomly wrote to agreed to give us five or six Saturdays of their time even though we would pay them under-award wages of $500 for the whole five days. The finiteness of their contribution was an important reason so many people agreed to be part of the process.

For local government, I think the citizens' jury experiment has been a great success. We need to become more transparent. We need to have more easy access to information. I think we should do more of these citizen juries for vexed policy decisions where there are trade-offs. They are great for trade-off decisions. I would love, for example, to do one on our enterprise agreement, which is 99 pages and has 1,041 clauses. But so far I have had no success in that endeavour, with the typical response being 'you can't talk about that'. The challenge with the citizen jury is to do it in a scaled way and keep the cost down per project. We spent $182,000 on ours. And though we would love to roll them out at short notice on various issues, they are very face-to-face, intensive, time-consuming and costly. These are all challenges for the model of citizens' juries.

It would be great to develop some sort of a model that can be scaled at a reasonable cost, because in an era of massive loss of trust, I am a huge fan of citizens' juries. Panels have now been tried all over Australia and they generally get it right. It is rare for a panel, after a deep dive, to come out with a stupid recommendation. It is amazing how smart the community is when you randomly select them. If you safeguard it with an 80 per cent super majority requirement, meaning nothing is approved unless it is positive and popular, and you put a real decision on the line, it is amazing how smart panellists are. To conclude, in light of the City of Melbourne's experience, I would recommend citizens' juries as a policymaking tool for all levels of government. Yes, you have to give up some power. Yes, it is a risk. But from our experience, it has worked very well.

References

The Economist. 2017. 'Global Liveability Has Improved for the First Time in a Decade'. 16 August. Available from www.economist.com/blogs/graphicdetail/2017/08/daily-chart-10

Reece, N. 2014. 'Putting People Power Back into Democracy'. 1 September, *The Age*.

Reece, N. 2015. 'Melbourne's Democracy Experiment Pays Off'. 29 June, *The Age*.

Ryan, R. 2015. 'Melbourne Citizens' Jury Success Offers Fresh Hope for Democratic Renewal'. 3 July, *ABC Radio National*. Available from www.abc.net.au/radionational/programs/sundayextra/citizens-jury-success-offers-fresh-hope-for-democratic-renewal/6589630

Innovation and empowerment in Finland: How citizens and technology are reshaping government through crowdsourcing

Tanja Aitamurto

In this chapter on innovation and empowerment in Finland, I will examine a relevant case study on the government's use of new technology to promote social inclusion through crowdsourcing. I will focus on three major aspects in crowdsourced policymaking: motivations, outcomes and challenges. The chapter will be structured in three parts. First, I will outline the government's perspective—what crowdsourcing in policymaking is, why we do it and how we do it. Next, I will focus on the crowd's perspective. To do this, I will take the user's perspective to understand why the crowd participates, what their expectations are and what types of things they are experiencing when they participate in crowdsourced policymaking. The final part of my chapter will focus on outcomes, challenges and the way forward in crowdsourced policymaking.

So what challenges do we face in Finland, my home country? In Finland, we have significant snow coverage for most of the year, particularly in the northern part, by the Arctic Circle. Up there we move around with snowmobiles in the winter. One of the local residents who lives in Lapland in Northern Finland is called Jaska. Jaska is a regular Finn living just by the Arctic Circle in a very remote village, one hour from grocery stores or post offices. Jaska uses his snowmobile on a daily basis: to commute, to run errands and so on. Jaska also uses his snowmobile to herd his reindeer, because for him the snowmobile is the most convenient way to get around remote areas in winter.

Addressing local complaints of citizens

A few years ago, Jaska was not very happy about where and how he could ride his snowmobile. The off-road traffic law governed off-road traffic—all the traffic that happened beyond established roads, like riding a snowmobile in winter or an all-terrain vehicle in summer. This law had been in place for about 20 years, but there were many complaints that the law had become outdated and should be reformed. The law had two basic goals: to protect nature from the harm that off-road traffic causes and ensure the safety of off-road traffic drivers and the people around them.

Jaska was not alone with his complaint. There were several stakeholder groups also complaining about the law; for instance, land owners. They were worried about the amount of compensation they received when their lands were being used for off-road traffic. Another stakeholder group were the Saami, the only officially recognised Indigenous people in Europe, who use snowmobiles for herding reindeer, hunting and fishing. They wanted special permission for using off-road vehicles.

Then, of course, we had the issue of individual snowmobile owners' rights (like Jaska's), and the value of conserving nature as it is, and every citizen's right to a peaceful environment. Imagine, for example, you have a cabin somewhere in the back country and you go there to relax only to be interrupted by somebody setting up an off-road traffic road next to your cabin. All of these factors were at play.

Some years ago, our then environment minister, Ville Niinisto, decided it was time to reform the off-road law. But he decided to do so in a new way, by involving citizens in the process; using crowdsourcing as a knowledge search method in the law reform process. In this context, by crowdsourcing I mean an online method for anybody to participate in a task that is open online. Anybody can participate by submitting ideas and comments online.

If you look at crowdsourcing as a phenomenon, it has previously been widely used for business purposes. Major companies like Procter & Gamble and Eli Lilly used crowdsourcing for their research and development, for example, through innovation intermediaries like InnoCentive. Generally, it worked like this: the company posted its particular problem online, and promised a financial reward (say $40,000) for anyone able to solve the problem.

There are precedents to Finland using crowdsourcing in the policymaking process. Iceland used crowdsourcing in their constitution reform of 2010–13. Federal agencies in the United States have used crowdsourcing in their strategy reform, including the Federal Emergency Management Agency.

What is common to examples of crowdsourcing being used to make policy is the process. It starts with the initial knowledge search and ideation, then moves on to evaluation (sometimes the crowd is part of that step, sometimes not). The next step is policy drafting, where, like evaluation, the crowd may or may not be included. At the end of this process, we have reformed policy.

Using the processes of crowdsourcing to invigorate policymaking

Let us return to the Finnish case, where crowdsourcing was used to reform off-road traffic legislation. A crowdsourcing platform was established. Anybody could participate. People were invited to submit their ideas in certain categories, for instance, safety. The question participants were asked to address was, 'How could we improve safety in off-road traffic? Please send in your idea'. There were additional questions about how to protect nature in a better way and so on. And the ideas proposed by the public would pop up on the platform, where they could be commented and voted on—thumbs up or thumbs down.

The first phase of the process we focused on was problem mapping. Participants were asked what type of problems and issues they had with the current law, and also with off-road traffic in general. That was called the 'problem identification mode'. I was involved with this initiative: after the first phase was over, we synthesised and analysed the input with my research team and policy experts in the government. This was used to design the second phase, in which we asked respondents to solve the problems they had identified in the first phase.

In other words, this stage moved from *complaining* to *constructing*, the stage of collaborative problem-solving. The third phase involved a two-step evaluation process: expert evaluation of the ideas by an international expert panel; and a crowd evaluation process. Then we moved to the fourth phase, which was the writing of the law.

Let us consider how crowdsourcing fits into a typical law-making process in the Finnish system. Typically, public servants write the bills of government, having taken their orders from the minister and the cabinet. The public servants carry out research as they draft the bill; they seek the help of interest groups and any expert committees they have set up to advise them.

According to convention, when the bill has been approved by the cabinet, it goes to the parliament where 200 elected representatives will discuss the bill, and then either accept it, revise it or send it back to the cabinet or the ministers to discuss it further. If this happens, the bill may be sent back to the public service for revision.

Why use crowdsourcing in policymaking?

How do we incorporate crowdsourcing into this process? The crowd adds one additional data point to the preparation part of the process. When the civil servants are drafting the bill, then, they would get more information from the crowd. In this way, the crowd does not touch the decision-making process, meaning it is still the parliament who decides the fate of any particular law.

This leads us to the very important question of what crowdsourcing is *not*. Crowdsourcing is not a decision-making tool or method in direct democracies because, ultimately, there the parliament wields the decision-making power, not the crowd. Nor is crowdsourcing a public opinion poll. This is because crowdsourcing is inherently based on self-selection, because it is only people who are interested in participating who will participate. It is not a random sample, and it does not have any statistical representativeness.

But equally, this self-selection illustrates the power of crowdsourcing: it is the people who have ideas who will share their ideas online. It is not an example of people gathering together to talk about an issue; we are not interested in their opinions, per se, but we are interested in the knowledge and ideas that they are sharing.

Why then are we using crowdsourcing? Because when we use crowdsourcing, we tap into the collective intelligence of people, and collective intelligence is based on the notion that when we have a large and diverse community—a diverse crowd—we are more likely to achieve a better solution than one produced by a homogeneous group of experts. When we use crowdsourcing, we extend the search for input from among the usual suspects ('knowledge neighbourhoods', as we call them in management science and engineering, meaning civil servants, policy analysts and experts). By crowdsourcing, we extend the knowledge search to the citizens' knowledge neighbourhood, consequently gaining much more diverse information that is based on people's everyday experiences.

When we use crowdsourcing in policymaking, it becomes a democratic innovation that brings citizens closer to the policymaking process. They are able to be part of something that they have not been able to be part of before. Why are democratic innovations relevant? Why should we care about those? Because, across the Western world, we are seeing a significant democratic recession. Voting activity is declining. Social cohesion is fracturing. Trust in institutions—especially political institutions—is decreasing.

I believe that when we use democratic innovations, and we try to study and apply them in an innovative way, we may be able to fight this democratic recession that so worries me. I do not claim that democratic innovations would take us directly to heaven, but I do feel we would be foolish if we lost the opportunity to use these new technologies and engagement methods to help people participate in policymaking.

One simple way that crowdsourced policy formulation already makes a difference is in the process itself. Thanks to crowdsourcing, we have more transparency in policymaking. We can divide transparency into two parts: horizontal transparency and vertical transparency. By horizontal transparency I mean transparency between the members of the crowd. In other words, the citizens. Because when people post their ideas online, anybody can see them and comment on them. That is horizontal transparency.

Vertical transparency refers to the transparency from the government to the crowd. When a government invites the public—the crowd—to be part of the reforming process, the vertical transparency is when the government keeps the crowd in the loop: posting updates about how the process will continue. This allows the participants to know the next step in the law reform process.

Evaluating the outcomes of crowdsourcing

Let us return to the Finnish example, and take a closer look at the evaluation stage of the campaign to use crowdsourcing to reform off-road vehicle legislation. When it came to the expert panel's evaluation of the crowd's input, we set up a group of international experts who received a sample of the posted ideas to be evaluated online. By this stage, we had received around 500 ideas and 4,000 comments. We clustered them together into certain categories and then established four criteria for the experts to use in considering the proposals: effectiveness, cost efficiency, ease of implementation and fairness.

For example, here is a proposed idea the experts had to evaluate: radio frequency identification tags should be added to all off-road traffic vehicles to decrease illegal riding. To do this, the experts used an evaluation scale of one to seven.

Then we built a new tool for crowd evaluation. We again invited the crowd to participate in the process and we gave them a random sample of ideas to evaluate. To do this, they would use three different methods. The first method involved the awarding of stars, which we called scoring. The participants would score the ideas based on their preferences. The second method involved ranking: participants were shown three to five preferences at a time and asked to rank them in order of preference. In the third, final method, participants compared ideas, as in binary decision-making mode, in order to choose which one they preferred. After this we ran some network analysis and found a significant majority cluster and minority cluster, allowing us to separate these preferences easily.

Moreover, because we conducted an entrance survey for all these crowd evaluators, we knew what their primary interest in the issue was. When we matched this information with our network map, we could see that the majority cluster was mostly snowmobile owners who wanted to have less regulation, and the minority cluster was environmentalists, land owners and, typically, women, who wanted more.

We then handed these findings back to the government for further processing. All our publications about this, including much on the evaluation process, can be viewed on thefinnishexperiment.com.

There is another law reform process utilising crowdsourcing that is currently underway in Finland. It concerns the limited liability housing company law, which governs apartment buildings in Finland. If you own an apartment or if you are a tenant in an apartment, this law relates to you. It affects around 3 million people across Finland. The process to reform this law is similar to that concerning off-road vehicles, with one crucial difference: it was civil servants in the Ministry of Justice who initiated this process. We recently completed the second crowdsourcing stage, and I can confirm the ministry is running the process successfully.

What does the crowd gain from these innovations?

The second half of my chapter concerns the crowd's perspective. We will revisit Jaska, and the thousands of other participants who took part in these two cases.

First, what are the motivation factors? Why does the crowd participate? Why do they voluntarily spend their time online discussing and submitting ideas on this topic?

One reason is that participants experience a strong sense of empowerment. For example, one of the participants we interviewed said that this was the first time in their life they felt they were participating in democracy and influencing the decision-making process. It feels much more real than simply voting for a stranger. Another participant noted that the easiest way to participate in the democratic process from a remote location such as Arctic Finland is via the internet. Up there, alternative means of civic participation involve driving long distances, which is not always possible.

It became apparent that participants feel closer to the policymaking process when they participate online. The process may be simple, but it can make a tangible difference to both a participant's life and their perception of what role they play in a democracy. We identified four major motivation factors based on data from surveys and roughly 50 interviews conducted with participants. Ultimately, the main motivation factor for the people to participate was a desire to improve the law.

Participants had specific concerns with the law that drew them to sign up on the platform and submit their ideas. These people wanted to learn from other participants, their peers and the experts who were present on the platform, answering their questions and sharing information. They also wanted to hear what others thought about these two issues of off-road traffic and housing company law.

We can say that these drivers are mainly extrinsic, meaning crowdsourcing is an instrumental method for people to participate in the policymaking process. And it's a method to achieve something specific, whether changing the law or getting more information about it.

But then, in the bigger picture, participation turns into an avenue for advocacy. It becomes another way to get your desires through. It is also an avenue to be heard and to listen to the viewpoints of others. And yet, interestingly, participants have a very low expectation for the actual impact. Despite the fact that these are people who are generally self-confident and who speak up (we measure self-efficacy), they understand that their participation in this process is just raw material for the civil servants to consider and blend in with thousands of other ideas. This fascinates me, as it indicates that participants—who sometimes spend hours on the platform—don't let their motivation to contribute cloud the realisation that their contribution may not make it into the final reform. And yet, they still want to participate.

Another aspect that we have studied closely is the deliberation and learning aspect of crowdsourcing. This is interesting, as we designed these crowdsourcing processes exclusively as a search for knowledge. They were not designed for deliberation, nor for argument exchange, such as with citizen juries and other deliberation avenues, where people come together in a system designed for exchanging arguments. In contrast, our platform is designed purely to extract ideas and knowledge from people. And yet, in spite of this, deliberation happens. In the process of reforming these two laws in Finland, participants exchanged comments, opinions and questions—some of which were answered by a civil servant from the Ministry of Justice.

Learning was occurring. From our perspective, it was predictable that participants would learn about the law from the materials on the website and from the organisers of the platform. But what we did not expect was for participants to, through the process, seek to understand other peoples' points of view. I consider this a victory in itself. Regardless of other results of these processes, I am happy if I know that the participants have learned to understand why somebody disagrees with them, or that somebody comes from a different perspective.

Consider also the demographic characteristics of the participants: Where do they come from? What type of democratic profile do they have? The participants were evenly distributed across rural and urban areas of Finland, and tended to be well educated, with the majority engaged in full-time employment. What was particularly interesting to us was their level of civic participation. Unsurprisingly, some of the participants were the usual suspects: the types of people who write to members of parliament and participate in town hall meetings. These people represented approximately one-third of the participants. But 70 per cent of our participants were not these people. It was valuable to us to realise crowdsourcing had engaged people who otherwise would not be civically active.

Achievements and next steps

In the final part of this chapter, I wish to shed light on the outcomes of these two processes, identify the challenges we have detected and look at the way forward. First, the off-road traffic law process. This was a successful process in terms of participation, activity and press coverage. But the process stalled in the law-writing stage, because the minister who initiated the process had to leave his position, and the new minister didn't care about the process. Unfortunately, as a consequence, all the ideas, evaluations and reports gained from a smooth crowdsourcing process are now sitting on the minister's desk.

For its part, the housing company law process is going very well. I think one of the key reasons for this is that in contrast to the off-road law reform process, this one is driven by civil servants who are hired for a substantial amount of time; ministers, on the other hand, have their portfolios shuffled and are influenced by political changes and reality. These two contrasting experiences suggest that where civil servants are invested in these processes, there is a stronger likelihood of crowd input being analysed, evaluated and ultimately channelled into law.

There are other challenges we have identified along the way. One is the significant conflict that exists between the logic of the crowd and the logic of policymakers. I am working on this challenge at the moment. It can be divided into different aspects. The first concerns the nature of the input. In crowdsourced policymaking, for example, the crowd's input is *atomic*—it can be scattered. This contrasts with traditional policymaking where that input is *coherent*: it is synthesised and holistic; it can become law as is.

In the case of the crowdsourced off-road traffic law process, many of the proposed changes were submitted without thought as to whether they were feasible to be implemented; whether they affect other laws that are related to the off-road traffic law, for example. We contrast this with the proposals to the law from interest groups, for instance, which could often be simply copied and pasted into the law if we so wanted. They also tend to fit in with existing laws.

This creates a significant disruption to the momentum of trying to integrate the crowd's input into the law, because it requires somebody to synthesise and evaluate all these small ideas and think about how they could be transformed into a more holistic form and channelled into the law. In this situation, from the civil servants' perspective, faced with this volume and diversity, they sink in all this input. To alleviate this, we need better synthesis and evaluation methods so that we can use policymaking-related crowdsourcing in a meaningful way.

Along with my co-author, Yale University political scientist Helene Landemore, we came up with these five design principles that might help us when we design crowdsourced policymaking: accountability, transparency, inclusiveness, modularity and synthesis. We particularly emphasise the synthesis principle because of the above reasons.

Another big challenge in crowdsourced policymaking is balancing preference differences among the many people that participate. These differences can be very practical: they could be about whether a road permit should be in effect for six months or two months. And these preference differences are not known before we do the crowdsourcing and evaluate the input. This situation differs from traditional policymaking, where the amount of preference differences is restricted to the ideologies of the various political parties and interest groups involved. In this scenario, the civil servants who draft the bill can anticipate the preference differences that will arise in advance, making it faster to channel that input into the policy.

But there are solutions. My background is in social science, but working with engineers and studying engineering scientists has made me view everything as a design challenge. To solve some of these problems, we are now experimenting with a new type of crowdsourcing. For now, I call it 'inter-credit' crowdsourcing.

As an example of this approach, I am working with the city of Palo Alto, which is the city next to Stanford University, to crowdsource input for their master plan, a 15-year strategy for the city. Earlier crowdsourcing stages for this resulted in many ideas from participants. And now we have launched a new tool whereby the city publicises certain ready-made synthesised holistic proposals perhaps to be included in the city plan, and then we ask the public to comment on them. We are doing it this way to make this evaluation and synthesising part of the process less burdensome for civil servants.

To conclude, I will return to what the individual gains from the process. Why do we need to care about the challenges and conflicts that arise between the logics of the crowd and the logics of traditional policymaking? Because we have people like Jaska who willingly and voluntarily participate in policymaking to come up with better solutions to our problems. Consequently, I feel it is both the responsibility of me and of the Government of Finland to figure out better ways to channel the crowd's input into formulating policy—be that synthesis, evaluation or something else. And the only way to do that is to conduct more experiments and share the outcomes in volumes like this one.

Part 3: Transparency and data management

12

Harnessing big data: A tsunami of transformation

Philip Evans

Let me start, if I may, with a story by Jorge Luis Borges (1954), the Argentinian poet and novelist. *On Exactitude in Science* is about an ancient lost kingdom, obsessed with cartography; the aristocrats cast one map after another of progressing levels of ambition until they launched the ultimate mapping project: to create the map of their kingdom on a scale of one-to-one. In Borges's story, the fragments of this failed effort can be found rotting in the corners of this lost empire.

And that is the end of the story! One paragraph long and classic Borges: full of metaphysics, and a meditation on the futility of human ambition. What I want to suggest to you in this chapter is that the image of Borges's map—a map on a scale of one-to-one, a map that is the same size as the reality that it represents—is the image we should have in our heads when we think about where technology is taking us.

Let me share with you some examples.

First, consider the Google self-driving car. It is aware of roads, traffic lanes, signals, and it is aware of other traffic. It is even aware of pedestrians and cyclists. In fact, in its first million miles the Google car only had two accidents, one of which was when somebody rammed it from the rear while parked and the other when it was being driven manually by a Google engineer. This is not wildly futuristic technology: within just a few years, these cars will be on the market.

But that's not the only way that the world could become self-aware and self-mapping. Consider a car park that is aware of the vacancy of parking spaces. Each parking space is equipped with a small sensor, which costs about $25, and is powered by a battery that lasts about five years. Using low-powered radios, these sensors form a mesh network allowing the municipality to collect parking fines when somebody outstays their welcome.

The extensions of this technology are obvious. Using near-field communication technology, the car can communicate with the sensor in the parking space, so that drivers can pay their parking fee automatically. Moreover, since the owner of the car park or the municipality then knows the exact availability of spaces, they can broadcast to the world a universal map of parking. In some major cities, 40 per cent of the traffic is made up of people driving around in circles looking for parking spaces. When the location of empty parking spaces is universally visible, drivers can book them and owners can even auction them to the highest bidder. We could massively improve the efficiency with which these spaces are allocated and reduce traffic congestion.

And of course, obviously, when the Google car drives you to work, it can drop you off and go find a parking space for itself. The key point here is that in this future world, the physical distribution of cars in spaces on asphalt and the electronic rendering of what is going on, become coincident. Traffic and parking become their own map.

Consider a third example. Nature's map of humans is the chemical structure of DNA. It took something in the order of 10 years and $150 million to first map one human genome. In the intervening years, the cost of mapping the human genome has come down with extraordinary speed. Quite soon, we will be able to map the human genome for less than $100.

Back when mapping the human genome cost $150 million, it was a very expensive exercise in 'big science'. And by treating just one person's genome as representative of all humanity, they abstracted from the human variation that is the essence of medicine. But when genomic mapping takes 20 minutes, and costs $99 while you wait, it is no longer a matter of abstract research—it is a matter of clinical medicine. Consequently, when you go to the doctor in the near future, the first thing they will do, if they haven't already, will be to map your genome.

The essence of medical practice in the future will become *statistical*, relating genomic data with other medical data: your medical record, symptoms, and ambient data from the environment. What used to be a process based solely on expertise, conducted within hierarchical organisations, where the final judgement was made by somebody with many years of expensive technical training, will become much more of a *statistical* exercise.

Already, Watson, the software technology originally developed by IBM to win the *Jeopardy* television contest in the United States is being applied to the task of medical diagnosis. Using statistical techniques, Watson is able to combine all of these data sets, including genomic data, and outperform 98 per cent of human practitioners in performing some radiological diagnoses. This doesn't render the doctor obsolete, but it fundamentally transforms how we need to think about medicine. In particular, our ability to aggregate, to standardise, to anonymise and to protect large data sets becomes crucial to our ability to use statistical methods in order to address these kinds of problems.

This is the challenge. It's a challenge in terms of the computer science and the mathematics, but it's also a challenge in terms of the institutions. In countries like the United States, where medicine is privatised, each hospital and each clinic thinks of medical data as proprietary. It's a 'switching cost'; it's a source of what they would call 'competitive advantage'. But preserving that data-based competitive advantage is of limited compatibility with large-scale data-mining of genomic and clinical information. As a result, we have a fundamental conflict emerging between the direction that the technology is taking us and many of the institutional arrangements that, in the public sector as well as the private, stand in the way. This is destined to become an enormous challenge over the next 10 years.

Consider my last example of how data can serve as infrastructure. Readers would be familiar with satellite maps of the United States at night, where you can see cities and roads lit up in the darkness. If you do the same kind of map for Africa, tragically it is the Dark Continent. The lack of infrastructure is one of the things holding back economic development in Africa. A few years ago in the Ivory Coast, Orange, the French telecommunications company and monopoly provider of cell phone services in that country, launched a project where they collected metadata on cellular phone usage for a high fraction of the population over a nine-month period. What resulted is an immense data set: who talks to whom, how people move around. Orange then carefully anonymised the data and published it (Palchykov et al. 2014), encouraging researchers simply to see what they could find.

Over 80 research papers were written with the benefit of this extraordinary data set. Data on how people move around, for example, shed light on the spread of infectious diseases. Warning people to wash their hands or boil their drinking water is among the most important methods to combat the spread of infections. But it has long been known that word of mouth is the most effective way to spread such messages. So the Orange data sets revealed not only the network over which infection spreads (people's movements) but also the communication network through which countervailing propaganda can be disseminated.

But some researchers at IBM in Dublin realised that this same data set showed the commuter patterns in cities. They took the largest city in the Ivory Coast, Abidjan, and extracted the daily movements of people from their home to their workplace and back. They then asked themselves the question: what is the optimal design of a bus system, given daily commuting patterns?

Mathematically, it's a straightforward optimisation problem, but in computational terms, it's very difficult because of the size of the data sets. To manage this, the researchers set up a Hadoop cluster, linking a network's computers to work in parallel. After some days of computation, they arrived at a solution. It turned out it was possible to reduce by 10 per cent the average commuting times in Abidjan without adding a single bus. All because of the availability of heretofore invisible data.

In a country like the Ivory Coast, data is serving as infrastructure. This data, about how people use cell phones in a society where other kinds of infrastructure are largely absent, turns out to be a source on the basis of which all sorts of insights can be gleaned.

We have a new paradigm here. Traditionally, data has been the by-product of linear processes, used close to where it originates to make local improvements to the process. But now data can be aggregated over very large (possibly universal) scale, and we can optimise globally rather than locally.

Used this way, data becomes a universal enabler: general-purpose, large-scale, high fixed-cost, zero variable-cost. Like roads or telecommunications, it becomes *infrastructure*. Data as infrastructure is open-ended and its uses are unknowable before the fact. It makes possible experimentation, innovation and technical improvements in things like bus routing that could not have been anticipated.

What's the larger pattern? It is, I think, the interaction of four very large trends. The first is what people call the internet of things, the proliferation of sensors. For example, the aforementioned $25 devices implanted in the parking spaces or the sensors used in the Google car. Current estimates are that by the year 2030, there'll be something of the order of 100 trillion sensors in the world. There are already in the world today 140 sensors for every man, woman and child. As the cost of sensing falls and the volume proliferates, every device knows and reports on its own status.

Second, all that data accumulates. This results in an extraordinary growth in the world's stock of information, which is doubling every two years—the phenomenon of 'big data'.

But data is useless without insight. The third trend is breakthroughs in artificial intelligence or 'sense-making'. Machines learn not from explicit hand-crafted models, but by brute force from immense data sets. Correlation substitutes for causation.

The fourth big trend is mobility. The number of cell phones in the world is now roughly equal to the number of people. And because an increasing fraction of those are smart phones, they are themselves sensors feeding data into the network. They are thus a huge source of data. But they are a principal means by which insight can be consumed. You used to have to go somewhere to get insight—to a 'library', for example—now, you can do your search from your phone or even your watch. Insight is delivered at exactly the point where it is needed.

Together these four trends are what make the world self-aware and self-describing. They are really recent and they are mutually multiplying. They are driving a tsunami of transformation.

How do we organise to exploit these technologies, whether in the private sector or the public? We see hints by looking at a company that is native to this world: Google. Google's search system has a stacked and layered architecture. When you make a query, it is passed through 'layers' of servers. It gets broken into its component pieces and finally draws answers from so-called index servers, each of which contains lists of every instance on the web of particular words (together with measures of the centrality of the source in the network of hyperlinks). These references are recombined, aggregated and returned through the server layers to the user. It takes a quarter of a second. An absolute miracle.

Now, notice a couple of things about this technical architecture. First of all, it is highly modular—divided into small and interoperable components. Modularisation is key to how we deal with complexity. Second, it is layered—each of these rows represents a different kind of functionality. At the bottom, infrastructure: 2.5 million servers holding lists of words; at the top, the customised, localised front-end facing the user. This layered architecture is fundamental, because it enables Google to implement what engineers call the 'end-to-end' principle: moving functions as far up the stack (towards the end-user) as is consistent with their efficient utilisation.

Therefore, if something needs to be customised, if it's experimental, or something where you're recombining resources, you move it as near to the top as possible. If, on the other hand, it's infrastructure—a list, a passive resource—then you move it as low in the infrastructure to achieve economies of scale and utilisation. The end-to-end principle enables Google (and, indeed, the entire internet itself) to finesse the fundamental trade-off between innovation and scale. You get scale, efficiency, utilisation of capital-intensive functions at the bottom of the stack, and you get experimentation and innovation at the top. And, by separating those two kinds of activities, a generative architecture is created that can scale massively and also accommodate experiments and customisation.

In practical terms, this means that if Google doubles in size, they can add another 2.5 million servers at the bottom of this architecture with little difficulty. Scalability at the bottom is essentially unbounded. And once Google has the architecture in place, they can produce new products, enjoying what economists would call economies of scope, by recombining the same resources into new products and services. And as they proliferate products and services at the top, they add scale to the bottom.

The top of the stack enables innovation. The innovation isn't necessarily done by Google itself or by any provider—it can be done by customers. One of the interesting stories of the last 10 years has been the way so much innovation has come from users themselves. For example, an engineer called Paul Rademacher needed to move home and found himself going back and forth between Craigslist for the listings and Google Maps for the locations. It was all very cumbersome, but he had the idea of hacking into the JavaScript that these two internet sites used, and synthesising their results to answer real estate searches in an integrated fashion.

This became a business in its own right: housingmaps.com. And it was one of the first examples of what we now call a 'mashup': a web service that combines information from *other* web services in order to create new value. When Google got wind of Rademacher's business, perhaps their first instinct was to sue him. But in fact they hired him to create application programming interfaces (APIs), to enable people with rudimentary programming skills to build their own mashups on the Google platform. The first API was for Google Maps. Google has since published hundreds.

Worldwide, something like 10,000 APIs have been published, creating the possibility of $10,000^2/2$ pairwise mashups. Most of those are meaningless, but there are actually 8,000 mashup businesses. The interesting thing about them isn't that any one mashup is a tremendously radical thing, but that 10 years ago, you would have needed months of work and substantial programming skills. Therefore, you would have needed funding, a business plan and a venture capitalist to sponsor your work. The barriers to doing this were huge.

Thanks to APIs, exactly the same thing can be done in a few hours. The investment required for innovation decreases dramatically. A lot of these 8,000 mashups aren't businesses at all—they're things that people did for fun; because they wanted to show how smart they were, or for ideological or humanitarian reasons. When the cost of innovation is just one wet Sunday afternoon's worth of work then the models by which innovation happen fundamentally change. You don't need corporations. You don't need government departments. You don't even need venture capital.

That's just one example of how innovation happens at the top of the stack. There's many others. Take e-lancing, the practice of taking freelancing work through online networks. Think Uber and Airbnb—both enable people to buy and sell services. Think about a commons like Wikipedia. Think about developer communities, such as the iPhone and Android communities. Think about social networks. Think about peer-to-peer networks such as BitTorrent or Bitcoin. All of these arrangements flourish at the top of the stack. Why? Because the scale is provided by platforms further down.

I will finish this chapter by summarising my key points in six headline propositions.

- Convergence of four big forces: sense-making (artificial intelligence), big data, the proliferation of sensors and mobility. Those four together create this self-describing world.
- Products become services, and services become systems.
- Data processing becomes infrastructure. This is the emergence of cloud computing.
- Less obviously, data itself becomes infrastructure: something that we build, release and allow the world to exploit.
- We see the emergence of new topologies of networked experimentation, innovation and customisation at small scale by very large numbers of people.
- And we see the emergence of horizontal architectures, stacks and platforms replacing traditional vertical architectures. Stacks replace value chains; maybe in the bureaucratic world, they replace departmental organisations. The world is repolarised from vertical to horizontal.

The managerial challenges that we all face—whether in the private sector or the public—are to grasp the scale of this change and exploit the opportunity to use information in fundamentally new ways.

References

Borges, J.L. 1954. *A Universal History of Infamy*. Buenos Aires: Emecé.

Palchykov, V., M. Mitrovic, H. Jo, J. Saramäki and R.K. Pan. 2014. 'Inferring Human Mobility Using Communication Patterns'. *Scientific Reports* 4(6174). doi.org.virtual.anu.edu.au/10.1038/srep06174

13

Government online: Are we there yet?

Tamati Shepherd[1]

To answer the question 'are we there yet with government online?', I would argue vehemently that no, we're not there yet. In fact, I would assert that if you are in the business of digital government and you think we are 'there', it is time to retire. Because you are actually never 'there'. If you look closely at the true nature of digital transformation, we are being pulled, pushed and driven by consumer expectations and social movements; by developments in technology and by policy change that means we have a big agenda ahead of us.

Consequently, in my department, Human Services (DHS), we have started a process that we call internally 'meerkat' reviews. What that simply means is, like a meerkat, lift your head up, have a look around and ask yourself: has anything changed? And if it has, change direction. We started this process because, if you read what we started to do in our service delivery reform agenda seven years ago, we did not envisage smart phones and mobile at all.

---

1   This chapter was written when Tamati Shepherd was chief digital officer of Department of Human Services, and is relevant to that time.

Thankfully, we consulted Gary Sterrenberg, the chief information officer (CIO) from ANZ bank, who pushed us in the right direction. He said the world was going mobile, that no one's going to have a desktop and that customers are not going to do business on a PC, but on their mobile. I thought he was crazy. But he was spot-on: mobile and digital has gone from about 5 per cent of our business to now being over 50 per cent. Had we stopped and done a meerkat review, we might have seen that coming. We were lucky we had a retail bank CIO who saw it coming and got us ready for it. This is a lesson for other public servants: convince your internal audit units what you should be doing is meerkat reviews. Our audit department is having a meltdown thinking about how they are going to assess us when we conduct these reviews.

The first point I wanted to make is not about public sector digital capacities but about our customers and the community. The fact is, consumer assumptions about the way consumers conduct their life are changing, and so are their expectations. In that regard, government is not isolated: increasingly, consumers want to do business with government digitally. So, what does that mean for us? First, it means we have needed to stop thinking like a government department and start thinking like a retail operation; our benchmark is to make dealing with us as easy as with a bank, so if you have had to apply for something recently you will know we still have a little way to go.

The second expectation is to be available 24/7. We work very closely with our colleagues at the Australian Taxation Office (ATO) and in 2014, when we first launched myGov and myTax, we both realised that we cannot shut our call centres at 5 pm on a Saturday or a Sunday when our new peak time is 8 pm to 11 pm. That's now when families want to do business digitally with us. As a consequence, we had to reorganise ourselves, get our calls diverted to our 24-hour call centre so that if a customer has a problem at 10.30 at night, they will actually reach somebody who can help them with an assisted digital service.

The third expectation is immediate responses. On average, our customers are calling or coming in to see us four times after they have submitted a digital claim because they want immediate feedback about its progress. Gone are the days when customers will put up with waiting 21 days while their claim was assessed.

Just like Domino's, where once you order a pizza you can track the order—received, being cooked, being delivered—we aim to do the same thing regarding claims. We are doing that with our customers because in the digital world, when a customer pushes the 'enter' button they expect an immediate response—even if our systems are not always set up to do that, nor are our staff paid to actually process at that sort of speed.

The fourth expectation we have found is that services need to be synced. When it comes to dealing with government in the digital world, customers don't care what level or brand or agency of government you're from. If they just want to change their address, they don't care whether you're from Queensland Health, Medicare or Human Services. They expect that once they change their address with one agency, every agency will know.

We are getting better at meeting this expectation. Nowadays, when we receive a change of address we can tell the Tax Office, we can tell Medicare, we can tell Centrelink. And we are working on synchronising other details like new licences. It is consumers driving this change: in the world of digital, their expectation is that everything is connected.

Moreover, there is a big shift underway with the launch of the Digital Transformation Office. It aims to be more user-centric, putting the customer experience first. The Queensland Government and Brisbane City Council have been leaders in this regard, looking at how this concept of the customer's experience needs to transcend all levels and all tiers of government. Because nowadays, when someone has a child they do not want to have to go five different places to do the things that they need to do around the birth of that child. The environment around customer expectations is changing. And from the Australian Government's perspective, the Digital Transformation Office is a symbol of this massive push to digital.

I will now recount our experience of these issues at DHS. The department has over 23 million customers, predominantly because we do Medicare payments, which touch nearly everybody in the Australian community. We make about 60 million phone calls a year, have about 1,000 service points (400 of them are ours and 600 of them are agents); we employ over 30,000 staff, and we shift about $160 billion in Commonwealth money through the transfer system annually. This equates to about a third of the federal budget.

In other words, when we tweak things we want to get them right, because there are big impacts when we make mistakes. As an organisation, in terms of our journey towards being better suited to the digital economy, we first went through a consolidation or amalgamation phase, where we brought all of the parts of the old organisations together under our umbrella. During that time, we did things fast: we built one finance system, one human resources system, one set of employment arrangements, a brand, a uniform for the staff, one-stop shops, and we got people co-training between Medicare and Centrelink and child support.

In the second phase, which is sometimes known as superciliary reform, we did a lot of work on integration. I want to point out a couple of things during that integration phase that provide interesting lessons in the digital space from the last four to five years. The first is the value of co-design. We spent a lot of money setting up a co-design capability in the department: the notion of designing services with our customers. And we keep getting better at doing that. It was a bit of a journey, but to give you some idea of the value that has in terms of digital, consider the example of our child support app.

If you are a child support recipient or payer, you are probably using it. How did we design it? We started it in Adelaide, where we asked our staff to brainstorm what would be the core thing we could do with a child support app, what would be of value to our customers. Basically, we tried to replicate what we were doing in the online PC space in an app. We mocked it up, we prototyped it and we took it to our customers and they said that is not what they wanted at all.

Initially we were adamant: we explained that it was simply what they were doing on a PC with us, just replicated in app form. And they said no, if government was going to use smart phones, they wanted the ability to be able to talk to each other via the app to make arrangements around shared care and a whole range of dialogue. Because, they said, if we have to do that on a government app, we will be nice to each other and, if you support that dialogue, and then do all the calculations you need to do about our child support arrangements, you can just get out of our way then and we will deal with that and only contact you when we need to.

In this way, the mode of the delivery reframed the service delivery model because when we put it in parents' hands, they saw the value of it being a bi-directional digital conversation between them and us. And now, we do what we need to do at the backend to make calculations and adjustments, only intervening when we absolutely need to. The whole experience was a good lesson in not assuming all the best ideas have to be in your own team. Because the customer actually has some smart ideas around how you might shape your products.

A second example I wish to share concerns an idea a junior employee had about wi-fi. He sent me a note about it through our ideas program. He explained that we want our customers to go digital, but we do not offer wireless for them. Our customers are some of the poorest people in Australia. They don't have data plans. They have no credit left on their phone and we wanted them to download an app. This APS4 employee simply requested we turn on the wireless for our customers. We have since gone through a rather tortuous process where we were granted permission from the security people to turn our wireless network on for our customers, allowing them to come in and use wi-fi. Our only concern is not to make this *too* attractive, whereby our offices would resemble a McDonald's, with lots of people going there simply to use the free wi-fi.

Another focus for innovation is the myGov shopfront, which complements the website. It arose almost by accident. The ATO had to get out of its shopfront in Brisbane. So did we. We thought, why don't we go digital together? Why don't we try and put an integrated service offer together? We had a vague idea, but not a detailed plan. We put butcher's paper up on the site and we got the staff and the customers to co-design the service delivery model. We are now a couple of years down the track. When you walk into that site, you don't know you're dealing with an ATO officer or a DHS person or a Medicare officer. It's all integrated.

When they visit the myGov shopfront, the customer experiences an integrated government service office where staff have been co-trained in each other's products. It was a case of being the house that Jack built: we had to make it up on the fly and organically grow it; from Brisbane it has now spread to Sydney, Adelaide and Perth, and in the process been refined. We iterated as we went, but if you were to ask us what was our blueprint for the myGov shopfronts, I'd have to resurrect the butcher's paper that was on the wall in Queensland because that's how we designed it.

The next phase of our transformation is critically important. Because while we have done a lot of good digital work facing the customer, our backend systems do not support the delivery that we need going forward. We need to upgrade these backend capacities greatly.

In terms of some of our actual achievements, the numbers look good. While we still have plenty of work to do to improve our customer experience (you only have to look at social media to see that), two years after being established, the myGov website had 7.5 million users. This will only increase. My personal target is to overtake the Qantas frequent flyer program, which is the biggest membership-based organisation in Australia, at 10.1 million.

When we pass Qantas, we will know we have achieved a good critical mass. It is actually quite hard to predict what the end game number is because of the way people are entitled to different things and the way new members come onboard, bringing a new population with them. In 2015, we had over 5 million people use our apps, with over 1 million documents lodged electronically. Working closely with Australia Post, we have stopped sending printed letters for a range of transactions. Instead, we send recipients a message to their myGov inbox.

So, what are the main lessons in embracing digital transformation and improving customer experiences? The first is to develop a culture of rapid innovation and experimentation. If you try to precisely design and prescribe everything in the digital world, it just won't stick. Instead, you've got to get out fast, have a go, iterate, try things, break things, throw them away and start again. Because until you actually get out there and start using things, you won't even know what the problems you face will be.

The second key lesson for us in our bid to digitise is to have one digital team. We rejected the notion of having a separate information and communications technology (ICT) business, and instead established a united digital team. Previously, the way we were working as a business was either to throw a pig over the fence and hope ICT caught it, or do some new flash thing where integrated business requirements were the cool tool—adding wings to the pig so that it landed more softly. But then some of my colleagues in the room would inevitably ask: why is there a fence? In other words: why don't we build one team, combine project teams, business, ICT and customers and redesign our digital products? So we started doing that, and our results have improved as a consequence.

The third lesson is to act across government. By that I mean reframe the way you think so that you start to enable a whole new across-government capability. For example, we got together with the ATO in 2013; there would have been about 70 Senior Executive Service (SES) staff in the room, we were organised into service channels and policy groups. We were sharing information, trying to look for points of intersection. We got to midday and we thought, 'this is a disaster, we're never going to find a point of intersection'. We reframed the afternoon to look at life events and to look at individual journeys; we looked at a small business and thought, 'wow, look at these points of intersection where we make people bounce in between us, let's see if we can change that'.

The integrated shopfront offer came out of that, as did myGov at the front end.

To give you some perspective, our technology platform in DHS was invented about the same time as Pacman—the same era as the cassette. Not many people nowadays would have a cassette in their ownership. Yet at DHS, we are still running cassettes: they run our payment system. At 30 years old, they are a reliable workhorse but not agile. But you know government: ask for a change, and nine months and $8 million later they will get back to you with a result. And so we are not really in a position with a platform that enables agile service delivery, let alone policy delivery.

When we started, the system that we built paid out $10 billion a year and touched around 2.5 million Australians. Nowadays, it pays out over $100 billion a year, meaning that it needs updating beyond simply the proverbial new lick of paint. And so rather than pour the same old wine into a new bottle, we decided we would completely rethink what the business model would need to be to support government going forward. A couple of key outcomes emerged.

The first is that government can no longer invest in an agency to replace its system for only its benefit. We moved the whole business case into the mode of 'this is a utility for government': it is owned by government and it will need to produce a payment functionality that can be used across all tiers of government—and, I would even propose, across non-government organisations. In other words, government shouldn't build its own payment system for people simply because it is responsible for giving out incentives. Rather, it should use ours and just front it. The idea of government as a platform—now this is one of the platforms we want to build.

The other issues are being able to move more quickly and deliver on government policy. We are working in three-month cycles, data in real time and real-time reporting. Traditionally, one of the issues we have is that if government asks us a policy question and want the data, we are a little like Sir Humphrey in *Yes, Minister*: by the time we can come back with an answer, the issue is irrelevant. But in the near future we will be able to get real-time access to data, which currently takes a lot of effort.

In summary, to shift from being a siloed agency like Centrelink, Medicare or DHS to becoming an integrated agency that can provide a platform upon which government can deliver a range of services, we had to reframe our thinking before we got to improving the technology. And so, right at the start of the process, we put down our pens and ring binders, banned paper and put all the agencies in the room and said: 'why don't you co-design the investment proposition with us?'

As a consequence, when we went to cabinet, each one of the six outcomes for this investment were owned by different ministers. It was so successful we decided we should keep running the whole program like this. And although it is in many respects life events–driven, we had to pull back and create the platform to reframe the thinking around how we might approach this issue; hopefully, when we get down to the actual doing, that's what we'll build. But we didn't wait until the building stage to consider how to get government to function as a platform and have the lovely people from Sysco and Telstra tell us this isn't how you do it. Because the only way to stop silos from forming is if you address policy issues up front. In conclusion, we have moved from a relationship with our colleagues at the Department of Social Services, from ring binders of documents and committee rooms, to working in a collaborative space in order to redesign how we are going to make payments in Australia in the future. It has been quite transformative.

14

Realising the potential of big data

Marie Johnson

We cannot discuss big data unless we understand the notions of convergence and context. The foundations of our economy are changing and being re-architected. In Australia, we have a new payment platform being put in place by the Reserve Bank. And, together with the banks, the actual architecture of our payment system is changing. 5G: just think about what will soon be possible with far higher transmission speeds. The World Wide Web Consortium has changed the infrastructure of the internet to take into account the internet of things. And as we go around that wheel, we see processing power and different types of models proposed. Government's response is usually intrusive legislation.

What will be the impact of this massive generation of capability on the basis of new infrastructure? Will it eat government service delivery, administration and policy? We should challenge ourselves. These are foundational changes happening to the very underpinnings of our society. Together with massive computing capabilities, this is driving a third wave that will hollow out many of the jobs subject to disruption through machine learning, algorithms and associated developments. Many of these jobs are found in the public sector.

In other words, we have two dimensions that we are dealing with: the re-engineering of the machinery of government, and what happens to policy and democracy when the middle class is hollowed out. To consider these dual issues, I will consider previous changes in other industries.

First, the digital disruption of transport. Once upon a time, a train would have been filled with mostly gentlemen reading their big newspapers; now all kinds of people are crammed onto trains and, thanks to portable devices, so much more is happening than merely being transported. The train itself has become a platform—rather than just leaving from a one.

The car is the same: from manual to automatic to self-driving, the car has become a data platform to inform policy. For example, Kandi is an electric car vending machine in China. You pay the equivalent of a few dollars to hire this tiny smart car, which descends from a lift, ready for you to use. Each Kandi contains a SIM so it can be located at any time. Users can rent the vehicles for an hour at a time, with the system one step towards China's goal of 2 million electronic vehicles on its roads by 2020 in an attempt to reduce pollution (New Zealand Health and Wealth Report 2014).

The modularity and interoperability of these situations is amazing. We must always look beyond our Western economies to innovation happening in other areas. Another example comes from Vietnam, where an anti-theft SIM card is being fitted to motorcycles. In a country heavily reliant on motorcycles, if one has been fitted with this technology and is stolen, the owner simply calls the bike, which both disables it and sends them the location of the stolen bike.

What is the digital disruption of power going to look like? Windmills will play a part (albeit not if some of Australia's current politicians have their way). Solar power, too. Consider the following scenario: if you put solar panels on your roof and install a Tesla battery, you can be off the grid. This raises questions about who owns the power and whether it is an asset for the consumer to sell. Instead of giving your power back to the grid, maybe you could sell your power back to the grid? This would usher in a completely different commercial model.

Consider now the digital disruption of education. Online education courses such as those offered by edX have surged in popularity as society has changed. Education is no longer the thing you did after school and then stopped and went into work. We are now learning continuously, in our own time.

At New York University, a comparison of the increase in college costs with the general increase in inflation has found the latter far outstripping the former. The value proposition has been demolished.

This comes in the context of Australia continuing to attract foreign students. When you put these things together, the question must be asked: what outcome does the Australian Government want? Does it understand these converging issues and could it be that in a few years our export industry of tertiary education will be completely hollowed out? Do we understand that?

Next, consider the digital disruption of accessibility. When we talk about accessibility, typically we mean websites and having letters that are bigger than one another. In the United Kingdom, Microsoft Guide Dogs UK are behind a catapult initiative looking to use wi-fi and information beacons to help blind people navigate certain cities. With the help of headsets, users will be able to access things like the bus timetable or whether there is a gap between a particular platform and the train. Those who have already benefited from this initiative say it has changed their lives, because it reduces their anxiety of simply moving around every day.

There is also the actual meshing of technology with the human interface to consider: I was blind and now I have bionic eyes. This involves fitting a blind person with a pair of online, camera-equipped glasses hooked up to electrodes that are implanted on the eyeball and feed the brain visual information.

Let us move on to the digital disruption of retail. One need only to visit deadmalls.com, a website chronicling the fall of American shopping malls in the face of online shopping. But don't blame the internet—it is the bloated business models that failed to change that has led to the demise of many malls. The customers are still in the stores. And there they are experiencing a deep immersive customer experience augmented by data.

For example, one of Tesla's greatest innovations is to sell their products in pop-up stores *inside* shopping malls, much like Apple does. Another development in this sphere is augmented reality. This is now an economic reality. In Singapore, I have tried on an augmented reality dress, a phenomenal experience. When you think about the levels of infrastructure that are changing to make this happen, what does it mean for us?

The digital disruption of retail will provoke the pop-up stall to become the pop-up wall. Everybody wants to have that customer interface whether at Australia Post or Volvo. In the future, when you buy a new Volvo car, it will come with a capability whereby, through secure communication between a deliverer and the car, your groceries, for example, can be delivered straight to your car.

The next issue is the digital disruption of information and payment. Consider the example of M-Pesa in Kenya. 'M' is for mobile and 'pesa' is payment in Swahili: under this electronic payment system (using pre-smart phones), when an exchange of value is communicated between two parties, the value is taken off the buyer's SIM. It is tantamount to branchless banking, and the wider Kenyan economy has flourished because of this very simple messaging service. I think M-Pesa provides a lesson about the value of simple messaging.

It gets better, because M-Pesa has become a platform. USAID, the American equivalent of AusAid, has been working with M-Pesa to deliver health information over this platform, specifically maternal health information, because typically Kenyan women own phones. This is an example of health outcomes delivered in context with economic outcomes. All this without using a bank. This is not about money, but about the exchange of information. Compare this to the BasicsCard, a PIN-protected card allowing access to income-managed money in some parts of Australia. This was developed as a new payment tool; many in government still think about payments as a transactional type of a process rather than as a strategic tool.

Digital disruption with the internet of things is all made possible by the changes in the infrastructure. Increasingly, things are implanted with sensors to communicate with each other. Take as an example the sheath on the heart with sensors that can communicate to the doctor information about abnormal heart movement. But how does digital disruption affect what is happening in government? In 1997, the Howard Government decided it wanted to address red tape and, particularly, the $17 billion-a-year burden of compliance. They came up with three measures. One, that there would be a single point of entry for business to government, the business entry point. Two, there would be a unique business identifier (the ABN). Three, that there would be authentication between business and government. What was not fully understood at the time was that these initiatives represented platforms. So how have we gone in the 20 years since?

Today, that burden is worse, not better. This is because in the year 2000, the Australian Government declared that everything must be put online, forgetting that what matters is platforms. In practice, this meant that in 2000, everything was put online but the government still delivered its citizens written documents and faxes. Fast forward to the year 2013 and the Coalition's policy for e-government said exactly the same thing: we are going to put everything online and you can even still have it in hard copy. The thinking has not advanced: we are still taking this agency-by-agency approach. The missing component in both 2000 and 2013 were transformation and the client experience.

As a result of that, federal government agencies did what they were instructed to do, spewing out PDF forms on websites. This accounts for some of that $248 billion. What does it look like? A scenario not that different from a 1950s train, full of men reading big newspapers. And when, like this, the digital and paper worlds collide, it is the customer that bears the greatest brunt.

For example, in Australia, a hairdresser requires 27 different forms, applications and licences just to run a hairdressing salon. If they wish to serve coffee, for example, they have to have a food safety plan. We know from standard business reporting that 90 per cent of the time any particular hairdresser spends interacting with government entails providing data to government. My contention is: what would that hairdresser's business be like if it were reversed—if government was providing that hairdresser 90 per cent of the time with data back?

One of the most phenomenal innovations in government, I believe, has been standard business reporting. I like it because it broke the thinking. It dared to develop a taxonomy that the software industry could buy into and map the product development of their business application software to this taxonomy. Then you have businesses operating software that can transmit reports back to government seamlessly.

As a consequence, all those forms on the website that the businesses would have to fill out and send back to government are now done machine-to-machine. This is an example of software eating service delivery. Of course, the problem is that because it is a platform but agencies are silos, not all agencies are buying into this. I will return to this challenge for government administration later in the chapter. Sense-T, out of Tasmania, is another phenomenal example of innovation. This involves putting sensors onto oysters to detect their heartbeats—a proxy for water quality. This information is transmitted in real-time back through the system. Otherwise, oyster farmers are required to continually take water samples, fill in a form and send it back to the department.

These are new ways of conveying information. But what about payments, which is typically what government does? In a world moving towards digital payments, plastic cards continue to proliferate. We need to think about payment as a platform.

We must keep thinking about what it is about operating as a platform and how that changes what we do. Take the example of online accounts, which are excellent. But how many accounts do citizens really need or want? The New South Wales Government recently established another one for citizens. But the more online accounts, the more online authentications will be needed. We are not reading the signs.

The last couple of decades have seen innumerable audits, reviews and reports that have said all sorts of things about information and communications technology (ICT) projects. We are not reading the signs because the very essence of government, which is data, is described in a jumble as all being 'ICT projects'. But they are not all ICT projects; there is no such thing as an ICT project. When we talk about big data, there is confusion around the assurance process in government when it is called 'ICT projects'.

Worse than this, the agency capability reviews, which are on the Public Service Commission website, tend to focus on data issues such as possible breaches. We are experiencing all these bad data issues, and they usually result in some sort of data breach. But in an era when the machinery of government is struggling, there was no mention of digital in the Australian Public Service leadership core skills strategy for 2015. It is time for a phase change in the way we are doing things.

When we talk about big data, we should consider the opportunity to identify patterns that may not otherwise be observed. Consider the case study of the Great Ormond Street Children's Hospital in London collaborating with the Ferrari Formula One racing team (Naik 2006). An unlikely collaboration. The hospital had observed clusters of post-surgical neonatal deaths in London, but they couldn't figure out what the problem was. They chose to collaborate with Ferrari because Ferrari is phenomenal at data analytics. Instead of observing common patterns in a race-car driver—called 'high-risk handoffs' where time is of the essence—Ferrari helped the hospital apply this technique to little patients. As a result, incidents of post-surgical deaths plummeted.

We need to relook at what we do, and ask what can be eliminated. The imperative should not be to put more red tape online, but to take it off. There are already some examples. Registration stickers have gone electronic, as have bank passbooks. Because of big data and analytics, there is an opportunity to look at things differently. What would government service delivery look like if Google designed it? Speaking of websites, why not forget them too? Because very soon, they will be replaced by virtual assistants.

I have Cortana, the 'intelligent personal assistant' on my Samsung Android mobile phone. She knows a lot about what I do; perhaps we could ask Cortana for help about interacting with government? In the future, algorithms and automation—of which Cortana is one example—will hollow out jobs like office and administrative support, sales, data entry and document preparation. Not all such jobs will be automated: there will be the opportunity to refocus areas in frontline service delivery where it is most needed. We need a fundamental rethink of the operating model and the machinery of government through the lens of platforms and data.

In summary, the most significant battle surrounding big data is between platforms and silos. We still live in an era of authority of the agencies, with public administration still practised as it was in the 19th and 20th centuries. We rely on ICT systems and policy frameworks that are clearly not working. We talk about data intake, data retention and data management, yet we still have data pay walls and intrusive control; payments are considered simply transactions rather than platforms. Without a capability architecture, we have duplicated investments widely.

We must update our conception of shared services, procurement and government's view of the citizen. In the 21st century, the architecture of platforms will become dominant. Data will be released dynamically. It will not be released when we are ready, but when it is. Taxonomies will be published. Data will be exchanged instead of forms. We have to think about the connected citizen, the connected society, and we have to move beyond the government's view of the citizen to the citizen's view of the government—where it is the citizen who has choice. When we look at it that way, we see that data for the last many decades, if not a century, has been a servant, giving information to government. It should be the other way around.

The citizen of the 21st is empowered with software and data. I think that will change the relationship between government and the citizen in a way that government will not be able to control. When we see this divergence between platforms and silos—as with Uber and other instances where the consumer is empowered with software and data—we need to think about what the government and public administration response will be when we have a software-empowered consumer.

References

Naik, G. 2006. 'A Hospital Races to Learn Lessons of Ferrari Pit Stop'. 14 November, *The Wall Street Journal*. Available from www.wsj.com/articles/SB116346916169622261

New Zealand Health and Wealth Report. 2014. 'Electric Cars from A Vending Machine'. 30 January. The Main Report Publications Ltd.

15

Digital strangers, digital natives: Challenging the norm to create Change@SouthAustralia

Erma Ranieri

When I was asked to contribute on the subject of managing our workforces' generational divide, I thought that while I'm not really across technology, I am across the workforce. As the Commissioner for Public Sector Employment in South Australia, I oversee a workforce of around 104,000. In my chapter, I wish to explore how we, as a public sector, grapple with a changing platform for our citizens. In other words, how the public sector needs to set policy in the era of co-design, social media, big data, participatory budgeting and social enterprises. This is a significant challenge for any government—to start to think about how the institution of government, many hundreds of years old, has to change.

First, let me outline what South Australia has been doing through the Change@SouthAustralia program, which I have been leading, and what probably led to my being appointed as Commissioner for Public Sector Employment. Change@SouthAustralia arose from the premier, in collaboration with the Economic Development Board, declaring the need for cultural change in the public service. I was in another government agency at the time and was asked to come on board to lead Change@SouthAustralia.

The first step was to find people who can be innovative and make changes, irrespective of how old they are. They then, through a series of 90-day projects, were required to demonstrate that the public sector can find new ways of working; their projects were required to bypass the layers of bureaucracy and move into what we call digital by default. What was surprising to me was not that it was the digital innovators who came up with the solutions, it was that the solutions were co-designed.

None of these projects were done without the involvement of either business or citizens that were affected by them; together, we defined a problem and devised a solution. Often in government, by contrast, what we do is present the same thing in different formats: an app or a website that tells people what to do, rather than inviting them to co-design the solution. There is much to be said for instead focusing on systemic reform. We found, through these 90-day projects, the ownership of and solutions to a particular problem shouldn't just be the public sector, but include the views of the citizens we serve. But how do you go about obtaining that public value and engagement? You speak to the customers. That's what we did with the projects and, in doing so, explored the best solutions. We achieved some great outcomes as a result, some of which I will share with you now.

Perhaps the most important step was realising just how entrenched the barriers are around doing things in government. We have lots of really great silos. They're very healthy. So, we interrogated our procedures. We challenged the norm and tried to reduce red tape. And we succeeded. We identified over 700 of what we called 'simplified red tape ideas'. The problem is, the moment you start to unpack and undo that red tape, you get hit with more. Consequently, it's about saying 'I'm going to stop doing it' and so I've decided to stop doing some things as long as it's not in contradiction to the law.

Change@SouthAustralia has now completed 75 projects. With no extra staff. This equates to 75 (and counting) different projects that have been driven by people from outside of government suggesting what needs to change. This doesn't mean we don't still need the input of our employees for the process to be successful; we have over 100,000 at our disposal. Some of them have focused on digital solutions and we have used the principles of digital by default; we have noticed over the last few years that more and more of the problems we tackle are finding digital solutions. The outcome of this is that more and more public sector employees have a safe place to explore the opportunities presented by digital.

Sometimes, these solutions can become quite scary because, in fact, they are making jobs redundant—increasingly, the public can do things for themselves online that public servants would have previously done for them. Consequently, not everyone is going to embrace this sort of change. But the fact that Change@SouthAustralia provides an opportunity to fail—and the public sector tends to be afraid of failure—is one of its strengths. So the trial, in fact, was perfect.

I view any kind of program that allows innovation on the edges to be what I call a viral solution. Such an approach disrupts the norms and spreads new attitudes across the sector. Both of which we did. We have started to create a new public sector culture that celebrates innovation, seeks to find the best solutions and provides the best service; a public sector with a culture founded on the values that we spent so much time on. We need to then embed, I think, values around collaboration and about respecting diversity. Because if I'm going to get into the debate about Gen X, Gen Y, digital natives or digital strangers, we're talking about differences— and all of those differences are in the citizens and community that we actually serve.

All the Change@SouthAustralia projects use collaboration. You cannot do it on your own, it has to be with multiple agencies. We consult with industry, we engage with citizens and we integrate multiple reform tools. And it has to contribute to the vision of the state: it's not okay to do things that don't make a difference to anyone.

Consider the following examples of 90-day projects, completed with no extra investment. One is a real-time app that tells passengers when their next bus, tram or train will arrive and how late it will be. Another slashed processing times through the police and courts for minor offences. In another project, the Environment Protection Authority and the Department of Primary Industries and Regions South Australia got together and reduced the licensing period for tuna fishers from five weeks to five days. There are hundreds of other examples that demonstrate where and how we can do similar things. These aren't so much digital solutions as cases of talking to the people and the industries involved about what needs to change. In doing so, I like to think, through thinking outside the box and outside the traditional role of government regulation, we are helping business in South Australia to thrive.

Another of our projects centred on nurses discharging healthy patients. This started as another 90-day project and arose from the realisation that a criteria-led discharge was something that would save, in terms of productivity and time, a significant amount of money. Indeed, we were told the only reason it didn't already exist was fear over subsequent industrial action, either from doctors, nurses or paramedics. Everyone involved seemed content with the status quo. So the challenge for us was to think differently about what could be done.

We also had an Unleashed Open Data Competition project that changed South Australia from effectively having a closed government to an open one. This brings me to big data or open data. When we started, only two agencies were prepared to release their data, the rest deeming theirs too confidential to release. We sent the departments that had declined another letter, this one signed by the premier, saying we needed them to participate in the GovHack, Australia's largest open government and open data hackathon. This time we received 217 data sets from 27 organisations. So what is stopping us now that we have the data? What are we collecting it for and how do we put it to use? Ultimately, how can it best be harnessed to help government assist businesses and citizens to make decisions for themselves? These are questions we are attempting to answer.

Finally, let me fast forward to my role as commissioner now. How, in that capacity, do I ensure we work harder at our engagement strategy? It comes down to how do we, as a public sector, shift to where we need to be to enable greater, better collaboration and all that comes with it? Easier said than done.

The first thing I did was to reissue the code of ethics; one change we made was to consider it in terms of values-based decision-making, and start to introduce the challenges of social media and what it is to be in the public eye. By this, I mean what it is for citizens to find out about what public sector does, what it is to actually open it and start to set the parameters for people—whether they be digital strangers or natives. Ultimately, what we need to do is make sure that people are clear about what they can and cannot do, and how we can co-locate and work together in a new kind of setting.

That will not be easy as we try to move from old settings to new. We need to approach things with a new, principles-based approach, and I would like to emphasise the need to get rid of the rules that actually stop us from doing things. Solutions will come in new patterns of engagement; simple changes to how we engage with community, how it becomes almost the norm for us working in government, how we reflect those new ways through our workforce and are reflective of the entire community that we serve. We need to celebrate the diversity of that community. And, as a public sector, we need to consider how we can use digital to be able to give people the sort of information they're looking for. That way we can both have a positive impact on their lives and ensure we remain relevant for the next 10 to 15 years.

www.ingramcontent.com/pod-product-compliance
Lightning Source LLC
Chambersburg PA
CBHW041640050326
40690CB00027B/5280